gEt the gRammar

George Keith

Designer: Clare Davey
Illustrator: Nick Duffy
Editorial Manager: Barry Kruger
Picture Researcher: Helen Taylor

Get the Grammar
Published by BBC Educational Publishing,
White City, London W12 7TS.

© George Keith/BBC Education 1994
The moral right of the author has been asserted.

ISBN 0 563 39630 X
Printed in Great Britain by Bell & Bain Ltd

introduction

Contents

The notion of English grammar as a cure for all the language ills that today's pupils have inherited is only too familiar. The chief aim of this book, however, is to look at language in terms of good health, rather than bad, and to make the study of grammar a lively tonic rather than a prescribed antibiotic! Each chapter has been designed for use in conjunction with a television programme focusing on an important aspect of grammar. Pupils are provided with ideas and activities that will enable them to explore further a particular grammatical function or structure. The emphasis throughout the book has been placed firmly on the role of grammar in everyday, real life, spoken and written communication.

The book presents grammar in a systematic way, enabling teachers to fulfil the requirements of the National Curriculum, but the chapters need not be worked through sequentially. You may, for example, wish to link the chapter on verbs to work on instructional/advisory writing or on the use of argument. The chapter on nouns could be linked to readings of poetry and to the exploration of metaphors, symbols and connotations.

Above all, the activities are based upon what pupils already know about language (though they may infrequently reflect on their knowledge) and on what they are already able to do with language. Each pupil is challenged just that little bit more, which makes the material suitable for classes of mixed ability. Most of the activities can be tackled with confidence by less able pupils.

English teachers will, quite rightly, continue to carry out any grammatical repairs and instruction they can on any individual pupil's work.

The teacher's notes at the back of the book are provided to give teachers a framework for their own knowledge and curiosity about the functions and structures of English grammar.

The approach to learning about language embodied in this book is based upon experience gained at Key Stage 3 by the Language in the National Curriculum team under the leadership of Professor Ronald Carter at the University of Nottingham. The *Materials for professional development* produced by LINC, some of which are used in this book, have received national and international acclaim.

Life Sentences

life sentences

Sentence is quite a grim word. Like so many English words it has at least two meanings, one of which locks people away. This book is concerned about the other kind of sentences that we receive and give out every day of our lives.

> **I sentence you to listen to heavy metal records, eight hours a day, non-stop, for a period of not less than one week.**

That's a sentence in both senses of the word!

It makes complete sense, there is no doubting what it means and it does the job intended. Also, because it is a written sentence it begins with a capital letter and ends with a full stop.

But remember that punctuation doesn't automatically make it a sentence.

In this chapter you will investigate:

- **the four different kinds of sentence;**

- **differences in the length of sentences;**

- **some differences between spoken and written sentences;**

- **different effects achieved by varying the type, length and construction of sentences.**

Life Sentences

Look at the following:

Although we have been friends for a long time.
Because it isn't any good.
Bananas their carburettor beautifully fab whenever.

Voxbox

"Grammar is a set of rules that tells you how to put words together to make meanings."

"Grammar is (...) everyday English."

"What is a sentence then?"

On the capital letter/full stop rule, they all look like sentences but the last one is obviously only a string of words. There's no completed sense to it. The first two sound much closer to sentences but not quite.

Make the first two complete sentences by adding another half at the front or the back. Don't forget the comma.

When you have done this write a message with one half of a sentence on one side of the paper and the rest on the other side. Good connecting words would be: although, whenever, when, if, despite, because, therefore, unless.

Try to write something that will be a surprise when the paper is turned over.

Swap your piece of paper with a partner. You might have the beginning or the end of a sentence. Which do you think it is? Can you guess the other half of the sentence? Now mix up the pieces of paper to make other sentences.

A sentence can be as short as one word in the right circumstances. The word 'Help' written in the sand of a desert island would make perfect sense to a pilot flying overhead. 'Bananas', on the other hand, would seem odd; 'Although' would be downright mysterious. Normally, spoken and written sentences are longer than one word.

g e t
g R M a
t h e g a

activity

Unfortunately there are no planes flying over your desert island so you are going to have to resort to the age old message in a bottle if you want to contact civilisation. Imagine that your plane went down about 100 miles due south of Hawaii. That is all you know. You are allowed three sentences. What are you going to put?

Four types of sentence

Sentences can be very short and very long, and they come in different shapes. One of the best ways to understand them is to look at the jobs they do.

There are four kinds: statements, questions, commands and exclamations.

Statements

These tell people things and account for most spoken or written sentences, for example:

> **I like electronics because it interests me. I started to like it a few years ago. I took apart old radios and that kind of stuff. My Uncle Michael has given me a lot of help and some components. You have to have a lot of patience to do the soldering. I have made an electronic clock and have put it in a box.** [1]

These are all statements. They each tell you something. Statements are very useful for conveying information, ideas and opinions.

Questions

These ask something. They can do it explicitly by the use of question words, for example, 'what', 'when', 'why'. They can do it by reversing the word order, for example: 'You are happy' is a statement; 'Are you happy?' is a question.

In speech there is a third way of asking a question and that is by tone of voice. Here is a statement: 'You don't agree with me.' Use the tone of your voice to make it into a question.

Commands

These tell you to do something. They do not have to be as 'bossy' as their name makes them sound. There are polite commands, usually called requests. Sometimes command sentences are called 'directives' because they direct other people's behaviour. Here are some examples of commands:

Give me your hand.
Please keep off the grass.
Boil and drain the rice.
Even though you've fallen behind, never give up.

activity

Look at a copy of the notice in your school telling you what to do in case of fire. How many commands are there?

Find a copy of the Highway Code. That's full of commands too. Are some stronger than others?

Instructions usually contain a lot of command sentences. Write instructions on how to get to your house from school.

Exclamations

These call or cry out. They express feeling in a direct way and don't expect a response in the way that statements, questions and commands do. Here are some examples:

Cor!
Oh what a beautiful morning!
Hooray!
Great balls of fire!

Exclamations are more likely to occur in speech than in writing, though they occur in poetry, drama and in dialogue in novels. They would look very unusual in a textbook.

Even though they seem limited, compared with the others, they are so different that they form a class of their own. Greetings could be included, for example, 'Hi', 'Cheers'.

activity

Collect as many sentences as you can from different sources, and sort them out into statements, questions, commands and exclamations. Find several examples of the first three and see how you get on with exclamations.

Interesting places to look are: newspaper headlines, adverts, notices, T-shirts, badges, greetings cards, love hearts, graffiti, notices, a play by Shakespeare, a poetry anthology.

Make 'sentence posters' out of your best examples. You could make separate posters for each kind of sentence.

Driver's sick sor saves him from jail

Firemen's sale

New health unit to tackle council employees' stress

It's their birthday

Year's last Green Express heading for Blackpool

activity

Collect texts that will give you examples of statement, question and command sentences, for example:

- statements: any kind of information book or public notice;

- questions: school textbooks, application or official forms;

- commands: recipe books, instruction manuals, advisory leaflets.

Newspapers are great sources of data since they are full of sentences. Look at a daily paper and search for examples of the four different types. You could also work out an average length. Are sentences in *The Independent* longer than those in the *Daily Mail* or *The Sun*?

Select four or five good examples of each kind of sentence.

TO USE PHOTOCOPIER PRESS ON/OFF SWITCH AND INSERT COIN(S) IN SLOT AND WAIT FOR GREEN "READY" LIGHT THEN PLACE ORIGINAL FACE DOWN AND LENGTHWAYS ON GLASS AND ADJUST LIGHT/DARK SETTING THEN SET NUMBER OF COPIES REQUIRED AND PAPER SIZE THEN PRESS GREEN BUTTON AND IF AN ERROR OCCURS PRESS "CANCEL" AND RESET CONTROLS AND PROCEED AS DESCRIBED ABOVE.

Some statistics

How long is the average sentence? Find out by working out the average length of your own sentences over the last three or four pieces of writing you have done in English.

If averages for everybody in the class are then averaged, you will get an interesting statistic about written sentences.

Now look to see what makes some sentences longer than the average. Are there sometimes too many 'ands'? This is one way of making a sentence go on for ever if you decide to. What actually happens is that the writer uses the 'ands' and the 'thens' to join up shorter sentences.

Finally, look at someone else's writing in your class and select a sentence which works well. Say why you chose that sentence.

All the sentences collected could be displayed under the heading 'Best Sentences of the Year'.

Sentences at work

Sentences in speech are not quite as 'tidy' as sentences in writing, nor could or should they be because speech is quite a different activity.

Nevertheless, spoken sentences will fall into one of the four types.

activity

Tape record a stretch of speech involving two or three people. Find an opportunity when the talk is natural and fairly free flowing: at the table; a group discussion in the classroom; friends chatting.

Here is an example. Four switchboard operators in a hospital are carrying on a conversation about going out for a meal in between taking telephone calls.

Op 4: Good afternoon, Bristol Royal Infirmary.

Op 2: King Oliver's Cheeseburgers Blues, er, spare ribs.

Op 3: Yes, but I don't like spare ribs.

Op 1: Good afternoon, Bristol Royal Infirmary. Can I help you? You want Mr Smith's secretary? Hold the line.

Op 4: What did you have last time?

Op 1: I think I had the ribs, spare ribs. I'm not sure, but I didn't like them much.

Op 2: Mississippi Steam Boat Special — Switchboard. Yeah, what number?

Op 3: Oh, I had ice cream and everyone was giving me their ice creams.

Op 2: Umm…and Sally's favourite, her desserts, there's chocolate fudge cake. [*She is looking at a menu.*]

Op 1: I didn't like…I didn't like the pianist. Good afternoon, Bristol Royal Infirmary.

[*Emergency phone rings. Op 1 lifts it and listens.*]

Op 4: Thank you. Good afternoon, Bristol Royal Infirmary.

Op 1: Cardiac arrest, casualty! Cardiac arrest, casualty! ₂

This conversation has been copied exactly as it was spoken, though some things are difficult to transcribe, for example, tone of voice and the fact that two or three people will sometimes speak at once. Some sentences will seem incomplete because it is often not necessary to complete everything, especially in friendly conversations. Nevertheless, people still use one or other of the four kinds of sentence.

Find an example of each kind of sentence in the switchboard operators' dialogue.

Is one kind more frequent than the others? Which? Why do you think this is?

What kind of sentences are greetings?

The last sentence is particularly dramatic. It's an exclamation, in the sense that she is calling out, but she's not just expressing her own feelings. What else does it do? Notice too that it is repeated. Why do you think it is repeated?

What things do you notice in this conversation that make everyday speech different from writing?

Texts

However ingenious or economical we are with single or very brief sentences, there is no doubt about the need for longer ones to give us scope for what we want to say, exactly how we want to say it.

Here is a draft of a pamphlet written as a piece of English Language coursework by somebody who knows about eczema, a complaint that receives little publicity.

> **Robert is reaching out for your help.**
> **Imagine trying to tell him it's only eczema.**
> **Imagine you had eczema.**
> **Imagine waking up bleeding because you can't stop scratching, even in your sleep.**
> **Imagine your skin on fire.**
> **Imagine your skin stretched so stiff and sore you couldn't smile even if you wanted to.**
> **Like Robert, you would not be the only one facing these problems.**
> **One in ten babies, children, teenagers and adults in the UK has eczema.**
> **Some are lucky and only suffer mild symptoms.**
> **Others have to learn to cope with almost unbearable pain and irritation.**

Many become increasingly depressed and isolated.
There is as yet no cure.
But with your support there is hope.
Please give your help to raise funds. ₃

1. What is the writer trying to do in this passage?

2. What two kinds of sentence does she use?

3. Why has she chosen these kinds of sentence?

4. What do you notice about the different ways she has chosen to use these sentences? Try looking at:

   - length of sentences

   - order of the sentences

   - repeated words and phrases

5. Why is it important that she has punctuated sentences carefully?

Here is a piece of writing from a textbook on psychology. What do you notice about the length and shape of the different sentences in it?

For several years in the late 1700s, people living in and around the Caune Woods of Aveyron, France, reported sighting a wild boy running naked with the animals. After repeated attempts, hunters were able to capture the boy, who had been lost or abandoned by his parents at a very early age and had grown to the age of about 11 with only animals as his family. This wild boy of Aveyron was sent to Paris. Scientists there expected to observe a human in a pure state of nature, and after a year or so of intense education, they also expected that the boy would be able to tell them about his life in the wild and about the activities of animals in their natural environment. What the researchers found was a dirty, frightened creature who crawled and trotted like a wild animal, who would eat the filthiest of garbage, and who preferred raw to cooked meat. He spent most of his time rocking back and forth and would snarl and attack anyone who tried to touch him. The scientists worked with the boy for more than ten years but they were able to produce only minor

changes in his behaviour. He never learned to speak and his social behaviour remained so backward that he was never able to live unguarded among other people. [4]

1. Do you think the sentences here are fairly long, long or very long? (Compare them to some of your own sentences.) Why do you think this is?

2. What kind of sentences are they: statements? commands? questions? exclamations?

3. Where and why have commas been used?

4. Rewrite this passage as a story for younger children. Think about the type and length of sentences you might use.

Soap and Away

EPISODE 1

Here is the opening to Episode 1 of a satirical version of an Australian programme called *Soap and Away*, by Andrew Bernhardt.

[Open with shot of room with a home gym installed. CRAIG is sweatily working out with weights. He is wearing a singlet, shorts, shades and new trainers.]

[The door bursts open, enter CHARLENE.]

CHARLENE   Craig, we've got to talk.

CRAIG   I think it's all been said Charlene.

CHARLENE   You're not the guy you used to be… You've changed.

CRAIG   I've moved on Charlene.

CHARLENE   Craig, there's something wrong. It's like there's this…barrier between us.

[Craig's response is to work out more vigorously.]

CHARLENE   Craig, somewhere deep down inside you're hurting. I could help you, I know I could. If you'd just let me in…

CRAIG   There are some things, Charlene, that a guy just has to keep to himself.

CHARLENE   It's all over between Bruce and me.

CRAIG   As far as I'm concerned, Bruce is geography… er, no, the other one …history.

CHARLENE   Ever since Bruce's 21st you've been different. Craig something's happened to us. I'm going to find out what's bothering you if it takes me the rest of my life.

The script continues using the following types of sentences:

CHARLENE	question
CRAIG	question
CHARLENE	command
	statement
CRAIG	question
CHARLENE	command
CRAIG	question
	statement

Using the guideline above, write the dialogue that might have taken place. Put in stage directions where you think necessary. When you have done your own version, compare it with Andrew Bernhardt's given on p.44.

Hints: it's a good avoidance technique to answer a question with a question. How will you end your scene? The last statement needs to be carefully chosen if it is to have a good effect.

activity

Write a scene of your own using all four kinds of sentence. You could set your scene at a bus stop, or in someone's office during a telling off, or at home during an argument, or anywhere you choose.

As you plan your conversation, consider some of the following:

- who asks questions? are they just being nosy?

- who uses command sentences? do bossy people use more commands?

- who makes a statement that is really a polite command, for example: 'Somebody will have to do without.'

- who asks a question that is really a command, for example: 'Will you get out of my way?'

- who exclaims? is this a strong or a weak thing to do? does it depend?

- when are brief sentences spoken?

- when are long sentences spoken? by whom?

- who speaks first? who has the last word?

- who is in charge of the conversation?

- how polite/fairly polite/impolite is the turn-taking?

In this chapter you have looked at some uses of English sentences. In your own listening and reading, look out for:

- **which types of sentence are being used.**

- **how they are constructed.**

- **what effect a particular sentence is having on you (what does it make you think? feel? do?).**

In your speaking and writing, think sometimes:

- **is my sentence having the effect I want it to have?**

- **have I explained myself sufficiently?**

- **(in writing) am I using words and phrases more suited to speech?**

- **(in writing) have I helped the reader by using a comma where necessary? or any other appropriate punctuation?**

names and things

names and things

In this chapter you will investigate:

- **the importance of nouns for every aspect of daily life;**

- **the different kinds of nouns used in English;**

- **some other kinds of words closely related to nouns.**

Nouns are a class of words containing all the words that can be used to name persons, places and things. The word 'noun' is itself a name for the vast number of words in the English language that tell you what everything is called.

It is not surprising that nouns are the biggest group of words in a language. When you learn a new language you have to learn an almost completely different set of nouns before you can talk about things in that language.

There are three other kinds of words closely related to nouns. Every time you find a noun in use, one of these words will not be very far away.

They are all easy to understand:

- pronouns, which stand instead of nouns (for example, '**it**' for 'car'; '**her**' for 'Anne'; '**he**' for 'John');

- adjectives, which describe nouns (for example, '**black** car'; '**young** Anne'; '**big** John');

- articles, of which there are only two in English ('the' and 'a' or 'an'). One is called the definite article, the other the indefinite article. Which do you think is which, and why do you think they are given these names?

First, let's look at nouns.

Baby talk

From very early on in life, babies begin to acquire a stock of names for persons, places and things: mama, dada, teddy, milk, ball, car, MyMy (meaning Michael), bikkie, dodo (meaning 'dog'), and so on. Their repertoire of nouns grows very quickly indeed. A very frequent question young children ask is: 'What's it called?'

What do you think your first five nouns might have been? See if anyone in your family can remember.

Make a list of about 20 nouns that would name the most immediate things in a very young child's world.

Why do you think nouns are learned so early? Do you know any special family names or made-up words for everyday things?

Some nouns are very difficult for young children to pronounce, but because they need them, they do their best (for example, fid = refrigerator). See if you can find or remember some examples of your own. Are there any particular letters or combinations of letters that cause problems?

What's in a name?

Nouns can be subdivided into two groups: proper nouns and common nouns.

Proper nouns are the names of persons and places especially (for example, Michael, Robert, Edward, Sarah, Barbara, Warrington, Huddersfield), but also of some things (for example, NATO, Egyptology, GCSE). They are names that belong to whatever they name in the same way that your personal name is yours and nobody else's. It is true that occasionally you find two people with the same name, but this is the kind of exception that proves the rule.

Proper nouns

Birth certificates

One thing that proves who you are and what you are legally called is your birth certificate.

Virtually the first thing that happens to you when you are born is the registration of your birth and your name.

No two birth certificates in the world are identical. If there were two identical ones you would have the basis for a good science fiction story or a mystery.

Names and Things

Activity

Look at the birth certificate. Whose names are on the certificate? Why are those names there?

What other kinds of proper nouns are there on a birth certificate? (For example, addresses). Write them down.

CERTIFIED COPY of an   ENTRY OF BIRTH
Pursuant to the Births and   Deaths Registration Act, 1953

Registration District						CREWE			
1965 . Birth in the Sub-district of CREWE					in the COUNTY OF STAFFS				

Columns :—

1		2	3	4	5	6	7	8	9	10*
No.	When and where born	Name, if any	Sex	Name, and surname of father	Name, surname, and maiden surname of mother	Occupation of father	Signature, description, and residence of informant	When registered	Signature of registrar	Name entered after registration
158	Twenty-second March, 1965 Crewe Maternity Hospital, Crewe.	Paul Justin	Boy	John Simon Dunmore	Janet Louise Dunmore formerly Phillips of Lemon Street, Crewe	Clerical officer	J. L. Dunmore, Lemon Street, Crewe	Twenty-eighth March, 1965	V. Wainwright *Registrar.*	

I,   Vernon Wainwright   , Registrar of Births and Deaths for the Sub-district of **CREWE**   , in the **COUNTY OF STAFFS**
do hereby certify that this is a true copy of the entry No. 158   in the Register of Births for the said Sub-district, and that such Register is now legally in my custody.
WITNESS MY HAND this 28th   day of   March   , 19 65 .

Registrar of Births and Deaths

Family names

You are going to construct a profile of the proper nouns in your life. Answer the following:

1. Find out how your parents came to choose your name(s).

2. Draw your family tree back to your grandparents.

3. Try to find out the meaning of your family surname.

4. Find out the meaning of your own first name, and the first names of others in your family.

5. Do you have a pet name or a nickname among your friends? Make a list of all the names you have ever been called.

6. Do you have a family pet or do you know someone who does? What is it/are they called? Why?

7. Are there any names in your family that seem to you

particularly old fashioned or out of date?

8. Make a list of the names of five characters in a soap that you like to watch. If you were writing a new TV soap about your age group in the 1990s, what names would you give your five central characters?

All these names are proper nouns and begin with a capital letter when they are written. This is to let the reader know that they are individual and different from common nouns.

Common nouns

Other nouns are called common nouns. These are names given to everyday things and ideas all around us and inside our heads. Every single thing in the world has a name. Things that you can touch, taste, see, hear or smell are referred to as **concrete** nouns, for example, fur, salt, cloud, bell, cinnamon. Things that are mainly ideas in the mind are called **abstract** nouns, for example, truth, greed, laziness.

First, let's look at common nouns that are concrete.

Concrete nouns

Dictionaries, old and new, contain thousands of concrete nouns. Many of them are the oldest words in the language, for example: father, mother, head, hand, arm, sun, moon, food, blood, day, night, fire.

Why do you think this is so? What other nouns would you guess to be old ones? Make a list and compare it with other pupils' lists.

Check your words in a dictionary that contains etymologies as well as definitions. Etymology is the study of word origins and their later histories. Etymological details are usually given after the definitions. Here is an example from the *Longman Concise English Dictionary* (1985 edition). It is quite a long entry, so part of it has been left out:

> *eye* **n. any of usually paired organs of sight; a nearly spherical liquid-filled organ that is lined with a light-sensitive retina and housed in a bony socket in the skull... [ME, fr OE eage; akin to OHG ouga (eye), L oculus, Gk ops (eye, face)].**

Voxbox

66 *In Spanish you always have the noun and then the adjective, so that in English you would say "the white house" but in Spanish you would say "the house white".* 99

66 *English grammar is different from other languages I know. In English we say "the table" but in Urdu there is no "the", it's just "table".* 99

66 *My family they call me Lucy or they call me Lou, or my mum will call me Lucille which is my real name and I don't like it at all, right! My friends they call me Lucy Lou, they call me Lucinda, Juicy Lucy, Lucy Poosie...* 99

19

The code at the bottom means:

ME = Middle English (English from about 1200 to 1400)

fr = from

OE = Old English (sometimes called Anglo Saxon; from earliest times to period of Norman conquest)

OHG = Old High German (North German parent of the English language)

L = Latin (an extra bit of information which gives a clue to why an optician is sometimes called an 'oculist')

Gk = Greek (another extra bit of information that gives a clue to why eye doctors are also called 'opticians')

You can see from this that 'eye' is an old noun with a history that goes back even further than Old English.

Activity

Look up the following in a dictionary and find the odd one out:

horse, house, knee, potato, fish, clothes, tree.

New words

Language is changing all the time. One of the most noticeable ways in which it changes is the introduction of new nouns — almost weekly! The moment new discoveries, new inventions and new activities arrive on the scene, the language acquires new words.

Sometimes new names for things are invented, for example, nylon, from **N**ew **Y**ork and **Lon**don Chemical Company, who invented it. Most often new names are borrowed, or existing ones are put to a new use. Look at these:

anorak, **borrowed from Eskimo;**
photograph, **borrowed from two Greek words;**
mouse, **the name of a familiar animal, but also a computer control device;**

mole, **another familiar animal, but also a secret agent.**

Science and technology have long been responsible for large numbers of new nouns coming into the language. Over the past ten or fifteen years Information Technology has generated many hundreds of new things that need new names.

Bloomsbury's *Dictionary of New Words* gives the following examples:

logic bomb = **a fault deliberately programmed into a computer system by a disgruntled employee of the firm**
ink-jet = **a type of computer printer**
hypertext = **a system of database storage that allows documents and graphics to be linked in a variety of ways**

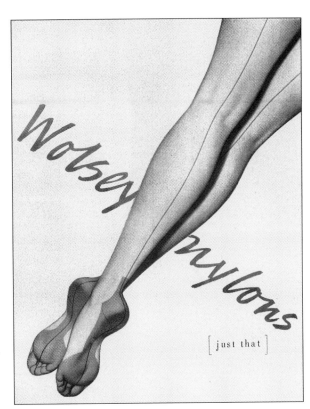

Wolsey nylons
[just that]

activity

Write down all the nouns you can think of connected with new technology and new activities in the following areas: music (hi-fi, stereo, tuner); sport (trainers, shell suit).

When you have made a list of about ten nouns each, look in your dictionary to find out where the words came from.

Which were borrowed from other languages, which were invented, which were old ones put to a new use?

Just as we import foods from other countries, so we import their names, for example, 'tomato', 'chocolate', 'onion'. Where do you think these foods come from?

- samosas
- pepperoni
- feta cheese
- croissants
- hamburgers

Abstract nouns

So far you have explored common nouns that are referred to as 'concrete', that is, you can know them through your five senses. The opposite of concrete is 'abstract'. In this section you will be exploring abstract nouns. Some examples include: beauty, passion, justice, ambition.

It is quite easy to represent concrete nouns. They are easy to draw, for example, and many dictionaries include drawings because they are more useful than words. But how would you draw a picture of 'secrecy' or 'love' or 'jealousy'?

The picture shows students in a drama lesson representing an abstract noun: 'isolation'.

activity

In groups of four, make a tableau to represent jealousy, love or greed.

Working on your own or in pairs, collect pictures and images from magazines and newspapers, then make a montage to represent happiness, loneliness and peace.

Abstract nouns are very common in everyday speech and writing, and they can mean many different things to different people. It is up to the user to make clear what she or he means by a particular abstract noun. Arguments frequently occur because two people have a different idea of the meaning.

activity

Write the same abstract noun at the top of three sheets of paper. You might use one of the following: aggressiveness, snobbery, unreliability, imagination, courage, loyalty, friendship, leadership, sexism, racism, religion, education.

Give the sheets to three people. Ask them to write down examples of what the word means to them and to write their own definition in one complete sentence. They should do this without looking up dictionary meanings.

While they are doing this, you should write down your own examples and definition.

When you have all finished, compare what you wrote. Look for similar ideas, different ideas, disagreements.

Notice how many abstract nouns have similar endings: for example, -ity, -ness, -ism, -ion, -iveness, -ship.

Nouns at work

Names are also important for making something appealing. Rowntree spent millions of pounds developing the brand name Vice Versas. Now the words (Latin for 'the other way round') have entered the language as a new proper noun.

activity

Collect ten chocolate or sweet wrappers. Look at the names. What do the names make you think of? Why do you think these particular names have been chosen?

What other nouns can you find on the wrappers? Divide them up into two lists: proper nouns and common nouns.

Naming

The names we give and receive can make people feel good about themselves or bad. Names affect the way people think about a person, place or thing.

Sticks and stones may break my bones, but names will never hurt me.

Do you agree?

activity

Look at the picture and at all the words in speech bubbles. Who might call the boy each of these names?

What difference does the name make to the way you see him? What nouns would you choose to call him?

Texts

Once you know the name of something you can file it away in your own mental dictionary of images and ideas. This means you can conjure it up in your mind's eye whenever you like or when another writer uses it.

Nouns matter to storytellers because they enable listeners or readers to picture people, places and things in their imagination. Look at *The Dead Pigeon*, a true story written by a nine-year-old and printed before the spelling had been corrected.

> **To day at afternoon play just when we was comeing back in to school Mrs B found a pidgin on the floor next to the Haygreen Lane side Some children had gone in but I was ther when Gary Destains said hay up thers a pidgin on floor. We all rusht up but Mrs B showted "stop come back and let me look whats apend to it poor thing." I just thout it was resting a bit but Dobbie said its ded it was when Mrs B picket it up its kneck just flopped over poor thing I said to Dobbie. She lifted it up with its wings and they were like big lovely grey fans. I didn't know wings were so lovely and big with so meny fethers espeshily When we had gon in we was just sittind in are class and telling Mrs Sandison and the others about it when Mrs B came and held it up with its lovly grey wings I was sorry for it poor thing and Mrs Sandison was sad and we all was.** Lesley (Year 5) 5

1. Find some of the nouns that you think are important to the storyteller.

2. Write a short story of about the same length from your own experience. When you have completed it, look at the nouns you needed to use.

3. Read a partner's story and compare the different 'worlds' you have each created by your nouns.

Nouns are also important to other kinds of writing. Now look at an explanation of the automatic train stop device, sometimes called the 'dead man's handle':

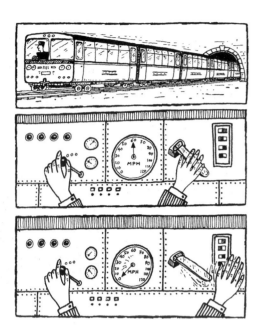

The driver's control lever in an electric locomotive has a contact attached to it, which, on being depressed, breaks an electric circuit. If the driver lets go of the lever for any reason, this circuit is closed causing current to flow through the windings of an electromagnet in a monitoring valve. This valve closes the pipe leading from the main air reservoir to the main brake pipe. At the same time another valve is opened which releases the pressure from the main brake pipe, thus causing the brakes to be applied to the wheels of the train, just as if the brake valve had been operated. When the driver's lever is released, the driving motor is also automatically switched off. 6

1. Find three or four nouns you think are essential for giving this explanation to somebody else.

2. Check in a dictionary any nouns you are not sure about.

Poets know that nouns conjure up feelings as well as pictures. Read the poetic speech by the Duke of Burgundy in Shakespeare's *Henry V*. The English and the French have been at war, fighting mainly on Burgundian soil. The Duke is trying to persuade the Kings of France and England to stop the war. Some of the words you may find difficult but you should be able to understand the general sense.

> My duty to you both, on equal love.
> Great Kings of France and England!
> Since then, (…)
> (…) face to face, and royal eye to eye
> You have congreeted, let it not disgrace me
> If I demand, before this royal view, (…)
> Why that the naked, poor, and mangled Peace,
> Dear nurse of arts, plenties, and joyful births,
> Should not in this best garden of the world,
> Our fertile France, put up her lovely visage?
> Alas, she hath from France too long been chas'd!
> And all her husbandry doth lie on heaps,
> Corrupting in its own fertility.
> Her vine, the merry cheerer of the heart,
> Unpruned dies; her hedges even-pleach'd,
> Like prisoners wildly overgrown with hair,

gEt
theg R n Mar
th g a

Put forth disorder'd twigs; her fallow leas

The darnel, hemlock, and rank fumitory

Doth root upon, while that the coulter rusts,

That should deracinate such savagery;

The even mead, that erst brought sweetly forth

The freckled cowslip, burnet, and green clover,

Wanting the scythe, all uncorrected, rank,

Conceives by idleness, and nothing teems

But hateful docks, rough thistles, kecksies, burs,

Losing both beauty and utility.

And all our vineyards, fallows, meads, and hedges,

(...) grow to wildness.

Even so our houses and ourselves and children

Have lost, or do not learn for want of time,

The sciences that should become our country;

But grow like savages—as soldiers will,

That nothing do but meditate on blood—

To swearing and stern looks, diffus'd attire,

And everything that seems unnatural.

Which to reduce into our former favour

You are assembl'd: and my speech entreats

That I may know (...) why gentle Peace

Should not expel these inconveniences,

And bless us with her former qualities. 7

1. You will have noticed that there are a lot of nouns here including a list of botanical and agricultural names. Many sound old fashioned like 'attire', 'husbandry' and 'coulter'. Check some in a dictionary. Even if you do not know all the meanings you should be able to tell if they are nouns or not. List them under different headings, for example: nature; war; peace.

2. Are there any proper nouns?

3. Can you find an abstract noun used twice with an initial capital letter? Normally, abstract nouns are not capitalised. Was there a good reason for capitalising this one?

Pronouns

Nouns make up one of the word classes of English grammar. Another of those word classes consists of pronouns. These are little words that can be substituted for any noun. They are: I, me, you, she, her, he, him, we, us, they, them, it.

When you do not wish to go on repeating a name, or when you are not sure what a person or thing is called, you can use a pronoun, for example:

John went to the dentist yesterday afternoon. Sadly, *he* **needed a filling which upset** *him* **a lot.**

This sounds better than:

John went to the dentist yesterday. Sadly, John needed a filling which upset John a lot.

How many pronouns do you think there are? Work them out for yourself. Note: one way of telling whether a word is being used as a noun or not is to substitute a pronoun and see if the sentence still makes sense.

Adjectives

Adjectives describe nouns. Sometimes they appear **before** the noun, as in:

black **car,** *happy* **days,** *big* **burgers,** *new* **friends,** *oval* **table,** *French* **pupils,** *Indian* **music,** *delicious* **food,** *beautiful* **view.**

Sometimes they appear **after** the noun, as in:

The sky was *black*; **my bike is** *great*; **the door is** *open*; **warriors,** *armed* **and** *savage*, **burst into the room.**

What difference does it make to put adjectives before or after nouns?

Adjectives can describe nouns in all kinds of ways. They can describe size (large), colour (red), shape (square).

Make a list of phrases or sentences with a noun and an adjective in each. Look at each adjective and say what aspect or quality of the noun it is describing.

Write the opening section to a ghost story that you would enjoy telling to your friends. Think carefully about adjectives you would use, and where you would place them. But be careful. Don't overdo it.

Very often adjectives are used to compare things, or to say which is the best. If, for example, there are only two things being compared, you say: 'This is the better one.' If there are three or more, you can say: 'This is the best.' Notice the use of '-er' and '-est'.

Look at the following:

> **fast, faster, fastest**
> **small, smaller, smallest**
> **kind, kinder, kindest**
> **less, lesser, least**

To use some other adjectives in the same way, you have to use 'more' and 'most':

> **open, more open, most open**
> **willing, more willing, most willing**
> **beautiful, more beautiful, most beautiful**

Notice the number of times the nouns are preceeded by a specific adjective in the dead man's handle explanation, for example:

> *electric* **locomotive**
> *monitoring* **valve**
> *driving* **motor**

Select some adjectives from the Duke of Burgundy's speech and explain what they add to the noun, for example:

> *freckled* **cowslip**
> *hateful* **docks**
> *mangled* **peace**

In your reading and listening, ask yourself sometimes:

- **where an interesting noun might come from.**

- **what a writer means by such abstract nouns as situation, problem, fairness, freedom, behaviour.**

- **what similar words (synonyms) relate to particular nouns or adjectives you have met.**

In your speaking and writing:

- **ask yourself if you are using an appropriate noun or adjective.**

- **make sure that you know what you mean by your own abstract nouns, and make sure that your listener or reader knows what you mean.**

Activity

Think of ten adjectives and decide which forms you would use for the **comparative** ('-er' or 'more'), and which for the **superlative** ('-est' or 'most'). Occasionally, both can be used in certain contexts. Watch out for irregular ones like bad, worse, worst.

Articles

Because there are only two articles in English, it seems odd that they should be considered as a class of their own. Nevertheless, they do a distinctive job and do not belong anywhere else.

They are 'a' ('an'), called the **indefinite article** because it is not specific, and 'the', called the **definite article** because it is very specific.

Once again, despite the small number of words in this class, they are used very, very frequently. In fact, 'the' is the most frequently used word in both spoken and written English.

Activity

How can both of the following make sense?

Are you the Padgate High School pupil?
Are you a Padgate High School pupil?

Is it usual to put articles in front of personal names? When might you say: 'Are you the Sally Jones?'

Do the following sound odd?

The honesty is the best policy.
A love makes the world go round.
The stitch in time saves nine.

'The' serves as both a singular and a plural definite article. What word would you use for the plural of 'a' or 'an'.

Soap and Away

EPISODE 2

CHARLENE	It all started at thingy's 21st whatsit, didn't it?
CRAIG	That's a matter of thingummy.
CHARLENE	You know Craig, I never had you down as a doodah pooper.
CRAIG	[annoyed] I am no doodah pooper.
CHARLENE	You know what's the big thingamajig with you Craig? You've got absolutely no doobry. [Craig, alarmed, sits bolt upright. He checks himself out.]
CRAIG	That was totally below the doodah Charlene Chandelier.
	[He lies huffily on his front. There is a tense silence.]
CRAIG	Rub some stuff into me will you?
CHARLENE	[Rummages around in the enormous collection of lotions and assorted debris.]
	The wotnot stuff in the brown doody?
CRAIG	For crying out loud, just rub it in will you?
	[Charlene sits up and pours brown liquid from the bottle onto her hands. We see the bottle labelled as 'OK SAUCE'. She rubs it onto his back.]
CRAIG	[wiping off the sauce in disgust] You know the problem with you Charlene? Underneath that cool, sophisticated whatsit, you're still a big thingy!
CHARLENE	Well I'd rather be a big thingy than a half-baked whatsit!
	[Exit]

Write out what you think the missing nouns could be.

Then, working in groups, write your own episode using the same technique of 'whatsits' and 'thingies'. Ask another group to supply the nouns you might have used.

where the action is

In this chapter you will investigate:

- **the part played by verbs in everyday life and language;**

- **the importance of 'being' and 'having' as well as 'doing';**

- **how verbs tell the time;**

- **how verbs 'would', 'could', 'should', 'might', 'may' and 'can';**

- **how verbs are used in headlines and slogans;**

- **what adverbs do.**

In sentences, spoken or written, you will find lots of nouns, pronouns and adjectives, but the essential part of 99.9% of the sentences used every day, anywhere, is a class of words known as verbs. Verbs are where the action is; they are the muscle of the sentence.

Some verbs are very obviously action or 'doing' words: for example, 'run', 'jump', 'walk', 'swim', 'make', 'lift'.

Others are less obviously actions, but if you think about it, they are still things that people *do*: for example, 'think', 'listen', 'smile', 'sneak', 'consider', 'like', 'hate', 'worry', 'hesitate', 'feel', 'try', 'guess'.

All actions need somebody or something to do them. Without verbs there would be no action. A verbless world would be a stationary world.

activity

A baby's development is often described and recorded in terms of each new thing it can do: for example, 'smiles', 'sits up', 'crawls', 'walks', 'talks'.

Ask your parents what and when were the verb milestones in your infant life. Design a chart from, say, 0 to 5 years, and put your verb milestones in order. Compare it with other people's charts.

List some important verb milestones in your later life, for example, swimming 100 metres, falling off a bike, winning something.

When you have done this, think of three milestones you see for yourself some time in the future, say over the next ten years. Try not to use the verb 'get' too often: for example, 'get a car', 'get married', 'get your GCSE'.

Picture A

Picture B

V ox box

" "Kiss" is a verb because you can kiss someone. But you can say "the kiss", so it's a noun as well. "

" What's the word "place"?
It's a verb.
No, it's a noun: a place.
Ah yes, but you can place something, can't you. It's a doing word as well. "

" Where I come from, people say "I ain't", "I likes toffees" and "Ta chuck". "

" What I need is a good listening to. "

activity

Look at the two pictures. What is going on? What verbs come to mind?

There are lots of nouns and adjectives you could use too, but this is not a stationary world you are looking at; things happen. Stories move on through the verbs that take place between the two pictures.

Think of the events that could have taken place to move the story on from picture A to picture B. In groups, decide on the five key verbs which took the story from picture A to picture B.

33

Remember: A word is a verb when it does the job of a verb.

Any word can be a verb if it is up to the job. Look at the following words:

elbow, hand, chair

Normally you would expect these words to be used as nouns, but look how they can be used as verbs in the following sentences:

You'll just have to elbow your way through the crowd.
Hand me that spanner.
She said she would chair the meeting.

Make up some sentences of your own where words you might first think of as nouns are used as verbs, for example:

He booked a room for two weeks.
You can't fish here.

The verbs that top the pops

Oddly enough, the two verbs most frequently used in the English language are not very obviously action words at all. They are 'to be' and 'to have'.

All verbs can have a 'to' in front of them. This form is called the **infinitive.** The infinitive is a useful label under which you can file all the different forms of the verb.

Under 'to be' you can list: am, is, are, was, were, will be, being, been. Under 'to have' you can list: have, has, had, will have, having.

These are the most frequently occurring verbs because not only are they used often in their own right, they are also used just as frequently to help other verbs. When 'have' and 'be' are used in this way, they're called **auxiliary verbs**.

For example, in 'I am a sea scout', 'am' is used on its own. Similarly, in 'She has a bad cold', 'has' is used on its own. But in 'Next year, we will be going to France', 'will' and 'be' are helping 'going'. In 'You have broken my watch', 'have' is helping 'broken'.

In addition to this, the verbs 'to be' and 'to have' often work with each other, as in: 'We are having a great time', 'We will have been to the cinema three times this week', 'They will have had breakfast by now'.

So, verbs very frequently come in chunks rather than in single words, for example:

> **You** *are being* **silly. You** *are going to regret* **it. I** *have been thinking* **about you. We** *are going to shoot* **you tomorrow. Your friends** *will be called to give* **evidence against you.**

Which is the longest verb in the above sentences?

Find three infinitives in the above sentences.

Now, take any book and turn to a page with plenty of continuous writing on it. Read the page and count how many forms of the verb 'to be' you come across. Do the same with 'to have'. What is the longest 'verb chunk' on the page?

Being and having

The verbs 'to be' and 'to have' are important in grammar because they are about something that is important in life. 'Being' is all about your very existence in the past, present and future, while 'having' is about all the things you possess.

Everyday sayings are often a clue to some of our deepest thoughts. Just look at the following, and notice the use of different forms and meanings of these two verbs. Explain what you think they mean.

> **'To be or not to be.'**
> **'The haves and the have nots.'**
> **'A wannabe.'**
> **'You've been had.'**

The time factor: tense

It is important in both speech and writing to be clear about when an action did take place, is taking place or will take place: in other words, the past, the present and the future. You will have noticed that the auxiliary verbs do a lot to help the time keeping, for example:

He *was* **quite good; he** *is* **now very good; one day, he** *will be* **fantastic.**

Time is referred to as 'tense' in grammar, and the time signals occur in different ways:

- in the auxiliaries: 'He was, is, will be';

- at the ends of words: 'She loved, she loves', 'They talked, they talk';

- and sometimes in a word change: 'I went, I go', 'I bought, I buy', 'I threw, I throw'.

Regular verbs (a huge number) add '-ed' to make the past tense. Irregular verbs (not quite so many) change the word.

Notice that the future tense uses the auxiliaries 'will' and 'shall'.

More baby talk

A very good way to learn about grammar is to watch how it grows in the language of very young children. Infants begin to acquire a sense of time only when they have lived long enough to have a past, and to have begun to anticipate a future. You can tell that young children have learned something about time (and language) by the appearance of the word 'when', which comes early in a child's development, for example:

When we did go to the supermarket...
My daddy buyed me some sweeties when we went to town.
It runned away when Chum barked.

activity

What do you notice about children's uses of verbs in the three examples above? Write down any other examples you can think of.

Next time you are baby-sitting or minding a young child,

listen carefully to the verbs. Observe what the child does and does not yet know about changing words and endings to form tenses correctly.

The case of the missing verb: implied verbs

As we get older and more confident with language, we can sometimes take shortcuts. When you looked at sentences in Chapter 1 you explored some of the occasions when it is possible to communicate perfectly well with only one or two words, neither of which is a verb. This is possible because the verb, though not stated explicitly, is implied. It is missing as a word but implied as a meaning.

activity

Look at the following conversation:

Boy: Home now? (= Shall we *go* home?)

Girl: Yes. (= Let's *go* home.)

Boy: Great film. ( )

Girl: Bit long. ( )

Boy: Fish and chips? ( )

Girl: No. Chinese. ( )

Boy: Hoi Tin? ( )

Girl: Mm, yes. A nice tasty take-away. ( )

Can you fill in the rest of the brackets? What verbs do you need?

It's the way that you say it: modals

Language isn't just used to convey the bare bones, the so-called 'facts'. Life would be very hard going if that is all it did. Language is also used to relate to people, to persuade them, to help and co-operate, to express shades of meaning.

I could...

You have already investigated one group of words that help verbs, the auxiliaries 'to be' and 'to have'. There is another group of words that help verbs. Their grammatical name is **modals**, which simply means 'a group of words that modify the meaning of a verb'.

Some examples include: can, could, may, might, should, would, must, need, ought. Modals are used when people are being polite, cautious about what they say, or giving advice or permission.

activity

Look at the pictures and discuss with a partner how each sentence might be completed, and the tone of voice in which it might be spoken.

The following pairs of sentences look very similar but the use of a modal verb in one makes a subtle but important difference.

You ought to...

1. (a) I swim every day.
   (b) I can swim every day.
2. (a) Give me a hand with this luggage.
   (b) Would you give me a hand with this luggage?

Discuss the different shades of meaning. Again, think about the tone of voice that would be used in speech.

I would if I could...

Whenever you want to persuade, permit, order, request, or suggest that something is a possibility you will find a modal verb creeping into your sentence. Watch out for them in other people's language. The presence, or absence, of modals makes a big difference to how people understand and get on with each other.

Adverbs

Adverbs are a class of words specially associated with verbs. They tell us:

- when the action took place (tomorrow, soon, yesterday)

- where the action took place (inside, all over, in front of)

- how the action took place (slowly, suddenly, unfortunately)

Notice that adverbs are sometimes phrases, that is, more than one word. Notice too that adverbs of manner frequently end in '-ly'.

Some adverbs are very popular in everyday speech and in the media, for example, 'hopefully', 'basically', 'actually', 'incredibly', 'personally'. What does each of these mean? Why do you think they are popular?

Sometimes adverbs are doubled up for emphasis, for example, 'very, very' or 'really, really'. Have you heard people do this?

Adverbs are also used with adjectives to make them stronger, for example, *very* beautiful; *really* happy; *too* strong; *slightly* open; *so* big.

Look at a piece of your own writing. Have you used any adverbs? Why did you use them?

activity

Working with a partner, discuss a situation in which two people are having a conversation. One is very angry at something the other has done, the other is extremely sorry. Write the conversation, using suitable adverbs. It could begin like this:

Joan: Right! This is absolutely the last straw.

Sam: I'm really very sorry.

Verbs at work

Headlines

Newspaper headlines are a very economical and effective way of communicating with immediate impact.

Argentina left stunned by humiliation

All-girls' schools top in GCSE

Minister to back two-wheel policies

Roman treasure hoard linked to sacked general

Activity

Look at the following:

Bereaved owners hope to join their pets in eternity
Boy racer 10 years old
PM eats own words
Athletes to boycott games
Islanders to go it alone
'My marvellous daughter'
Week-long nightmare for trapped teachers
Wrong baby hospital enquiry
Scientists predict new space age
Motor cars prohibited by year 2020
Australian bowling not cricket

Find three headlines that explicitly state the verb. Which verb is it?

Find three headlines that imply the verb. Which verb is it?

Find three headlines that use the infinitive of the verb. Is the headline about the past, present or future?

Now collect lots of headlines from old newspapers and sort them out into the following categories:

- past tense verbs;

- present tense verbs;

- future tense verbs;

- not sure.

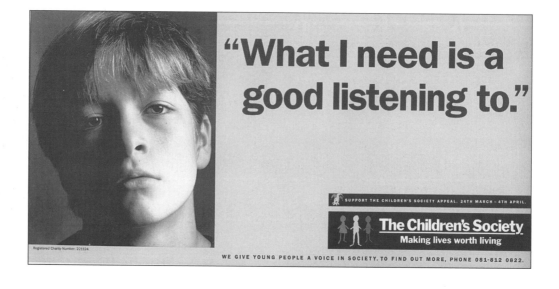

"What I need is a good listening to."

SUPPORT THE CHILDREN'S SOCIETY APPEAL. 24TH MARCH – 4TH APRIL.

The Children's Society
Making lives worth living

Registered Charity Number: 221124.

WE GIVE YOUNG PEOPLE A VOICE IN SOCIETY. TO FIND OUT MORE, PHONE 081-812 0822.

Slogans

Verbs make good slogans: they tell you to do something —
Stay cool! Belt up!

In one of the television programmes accompanying this
book, there is a news story of how the Children's Society and
its public relations agency decided on a slogan for their new
awareness and fund-raising campaign. They invested their
money and faith in a picture of a troubled looking young boy
and the slogan, 'What I need is a good listening to'.

activity

Notice the choice of verb. Discuss with a partner the
difference between the verbs 'to need' and 'to want'.

What difference does it make in the slogan to change the
more usual 'What you want…' to 'What I need…'.

The phrases 'What I want…' and 'What I need…' are
useful. Write down some of your wants and needs.

At about the same time as the Children's Society campaign
was being planned, the Multiple Sclerosis Society was also
planning a new campaign and they too were looking for the
right slogan. They decided on:

> **'If Multiple Sclerosis shattered your life, we'd be there
> to pick up the pieces.'**

activity

What verbs are used in this slogan?

Why have they used 'we'd' instead of 'we would'?

How is the second half of the sentence related to the first
half?

Find out more about the work of another organisation and
design a T-shirt with a slogan.

Texts

The tense of a verb is not just a matter of correctness; it makes a difference to the meaning and to the feeling or effect of the writing. Read the following passages, taken from the *Hutchinson Encyclopedia* (8th edn), and look carefully at the verbs. Ask yourself three questions:

1. What tense is being used?

2. Why has that tense been used?

3. Is the same tense used throughout, or does it change?

WRIGHT, Orville (1871—1948) and Wilbur (1867—1912). American brothers who pioneered powered flight. Orville was born in Dayton, Ohio, and Wilbur in Indiana. Inspired by Otto Lilienthal's gliding, they perfected their piloted glider in 1904 while running a bicycle business in Dayton. In 1903 they built their first powered machine, and on the 17th December of that year became the first to make a successful powered flight, near Kittyhawk.

DNA is a complex, two-strand molecule that contains, in chemically coded form, all the information needed to build, control and maintain a living organism. It is a double stranded nucleic acid that forms the basis of genetic inheritance in all organisms except for a few viruses that depend on RNA. In eukaryotic organisms, it is organised into chromosomes and is contained in the cell nucleus.

1. Stories are most often written in the past tense. Look at three stories to check this.

2. Why is the present tense used in a lot of scientific writing?

3. What tense would you expect in biography? Why?

4. What tense is appropriate to recipes, practical instructions, advice? Why?

5. Are commands or requests always in the present tense? Why?

Read the following, taken from a GCSE coursework folder:

I'm sitting in the launderette, waiting for a machine to empty. I always seem to be waiting for something to finish so that I can start. That's the story of my life. I'm only third in the queue this time. Usually there are umpteen people before me. Suppose I could get here earlier but I just don't seem to wake up fast enough.

I pick up yesterday's paper but there's nothing in it worth reading. Actress marries bishop. Who cares? Mortgages to be reduced by half a per cent. Big deal! My great, great grandfather was Jack the Ripper. So were three hundred other people.

A girl walks in. She's about my age and I know I've seen her somewhere before. Not at school. She's not from around here, I'm sure of that. Was she at the holiday camp? She looks at me and I can tell she's thinking the same as me.

'Don't I know you?' she asks.

I am thinking hard. Chances like this don't come every day.

In your listening and reading:

- **look out for interesting, effective or unusual verbs.**

- **notice irregular verb forms, for example, catch/caught, drive/drove, awake/awoken, wrote/written.**

- **watch out for other people's persuasive adverbs.**

In your speaking and writing:

- **think about the verbs you use most; are there alternatives that might be better?**

- **use modal verbs appropriately.**

- **notice the verbs you use most often.**

'Were you at Southport this summer?' I ask.

'Nope.'

She puts her bag down and sits cross-legged on the floor, real casual. I like people who can do things with style.

Suddenly I realise that I have come without any coins. Hell! Not only will I lose my place, I'll lose the girl as well. Still, like I said, that's the story of my life. 8

Write a short piece in a similar style. What do you notice about the tense? Is it what you'd expect for a story? What effect does it create?

Read the following:

> **ARIES: Between now and the full moon you will be laying the foundations for really getting on top of your life. You will need to be positive about day to day events and especially toward your friends who will be impressed by the new you.**
>
> **AQUARIUS: The news is good. Tensions you have felt over the past few months will begin to disappear. You will have a chance to build bridges and to pick up where an old friendship left off.**

Horoscopes are predictions, so there are plenty of future tenses here. But are they all future tenses? If not, why not?

Soap and Away Episode I *(continued from p. 13)*

CHARLENE	What are you afraid of Craig?
CRAIG	Who said I was afraid?
CHARLENE	Look me in the eye and tell me you don't feel anything. Tell me that it's all gone. Tell me it's over.
	[She crosses towards him. He is trembling. Is it nerves or the exertion of the dumbbell he is holding over his head? With one hand, Charlene effortlessly takes the dumbbell from him as if it were weightless. She pokes him in the chest with the free hand.]
CHARLENE	We'll have that picnic this afternoon, and you'll be getting the food together and you'll be giving me an explanation Craig Boulder or else…
CRAIG	*[pauses]* Charlene, can I ask you something?
CHARLENE	Try me.
CRAIG	Have you got any Factor 16? I'm really catching it on my shoulders.

Soap and Away

EPISODE 3

Here is the opening part of the script for Episode 3.

[Craig's room. He is waxing down his surfboard, eyeing its surface very closely. Charlene is sitting on the floor, propped up on cushions, reading a magazine. They give each other furtive glances. They are not at ease.]

CRAIG	Truce, OK?
CHARLENE	OK, truce.
CRAIG	No more interrogation?
CHARLENE	*[Non-committal, pretends to read magazine. Pause.]* Just one more question.
CRAIG	*[wearily]* Charlene!
CHARLENE	Just one.
CRAIG	*[sighs]* OK.
CHARLENE	Darlene Dingbat…
CRAIG	What about her?
CHARLENE	You and her…
CRAIG	Seriously?!
CHARLENE	Why not? Darlene Dingbat – Ms Beach Queen '93. Ace surfer, ace swimmer, ace sun-baker, *[acidly]* ace seducer.
CRAIG	*[affronted]* Darlene and me? No way!

What do you notice about this conversation?

Finish it in the same style.

seriously grammatical

In this chapter you are going to investigate:

- **the importance of grammar for connecting words together;**

- **the use of particular kinds of words to make the links;**

- **the ways in which connecting words help to make sense in arguments.**

So far you have looked at nouns, adjectives, verbs and adverbs. These make up the huge bulk of English words and are sometimes referred to as **lexical** words. This means that they belong to the lexicon, or vocabulary, of English words that have an obvious meaning outside themselves. They refer to things you can see, hear, touch, taste, smell, to ideas you can have in your mind and to actions you can do.

There are other words, however, that are quite different. They are known as **grammatical** words, for example, **articles** and **pronouns** (see Chapter 2). It is impossible to smell a 'the', or to do a 'they', or to taste an 'a'. These words do not refer to something in the world; it is their job to help all the lexical words mean what the user wants them to mean. They fasten all the other words together.

The meaning of English sentences depends very much on the order in which the words are arranged. A useful word to know here is **syntax**. It's a word that often frightens people but it is really very simple. It means 'to arrange in an order'. The moment you use two or more words in English, which is most of the time, you will instinctively follow the rules of syntax. If you didn't people would think there was something very wrong.

Look at the following scrambled sentences:

> **chips and disco buy the fish some after let's**
> **bike when your let will me you ride a have on ?**
> **team patch the the going bad through at is a moment**

It is not very difficult to put these sentences into a proper order, which goes to show how well you know the rules of English syntax. Watch out for the punctuation, though, if you write them down. Notice, too, how important little grammatical words like 'on', 'after' and 'when' are for joining other words together. Syntax helps you to do joined up thinking.

One way to appreciate the usefulness of grammatical words is to look at what happens when they are not used.

activity

Newspaper headlines frequently omit grammatical words.

'Angry fans demand cheaper tickets' is a sentence with a very clear pattern, typical of newspaper headlines:

adjective + noun (plural) + verb + noun (plural)

Write some newspaper headlines using the same pattern. The nouns may be singular or plural, the verb can be in any tense. Make your headlines funny, sensational, mysterious. Above all they should grab the reader's attention.

If you were to make a quick list of your Top 20 words, you might expect to find lots of nouns and verbs. In fact, if you look at the Top 20 lists you will find that nearly every one is a grammatical word, not a lexical one.

What do you notice about the words in the lists? Does anything surprise you?

What differences do you notice between the two lists? Why do you think there are these differences?

Why do you think 'he' and 'his' occur in the Top 20 and not 'she' and 'her'? Why do you think that 'yes' is more frequent than 'no' in conversation?

Are there any words absent that you would have expected to be in the Top 20 list?

Find a book with plenty of continuous writing per page. Choose one page and count how many times the top three words on the Top 20 list occur. What proportion of the words on your sample page consists of grammatical words?

You can see that lexical words have meaning in the world around us, whereas grammatical words only have meaning in themselves. It is impossible, for example, to find a 'the', a 'for' or even an 'it'. Can you explain what these words mean?

Why do you think that these words are so important? They are important because their special job is to connect all the lexical words together so that they can be used in sentences.

Most frequent English words

In the *Cambridge Encyclopedia of Language* there are two lists of the most frequently used words in the English language. One is a Top 20 list for spoken English, the other a Top 20 list for written English. What differences do you notice between speech and writing? Discuss with a partner why there should be such differences.

	Written English (newspapers)	Spoken English (conversation)
1.	the	the
2.	of	and
3.	to	I
4.	in	to
5.	and	of
6.	a	a
7.	for	you
8.	was	that
9.	is	in
10.	that	it
11.	on	is
12.	at	yes
13.	he	was
14.	with	this
15.	by	but
16.	be	on
17.	it	well
18.	an	he
19.	as	have
20.	his	for

Joined up writing equals joined up thinking

In this piece of writing all the lexical words have been left in place, but the grammatical words have been removed. Read it and decide what words would best connect the lexical words. You will need to use more than one word in places.

> — was always — breakfast — always — flask — coffee. — had eaten, — usually slept — corner — cellar — camp bed — Dad had bought. — morning was different. Try — could, — was — way — could get comfortable — bed. — way — lay — was — much — hanging — one end — other. — checked — see — was — different bed — some reason, — , — wasn't. Had — shrunk, — wondered? — had — wondered — cellar door yesterday. — full, sickening realisation hit. — clothes were getting tighter. — never seemed enough food — days. — was definitely growing bigger — alarming rate — judge — bursting clothes. — six foot camp bed — cellar door were — means — small side — were becoming — small — . Last month — had turned — teenage werewolf. Now — was turning — giant teenage werewolf.

Conjunctions

Different conjunctions do different things. Some simply link; others tell you something about the linking. The best known and most obvious joining word in English is 'and'. 'Then' is also used very frequently, especially in stories. Other conjunctions like 'when', 'if', 'because', do more complex jobs. They tell you more about the connection. For example, 'because' tells you the reason; 'if' tells you that there is a condition attached.

Prepositions

A lot of the missing words above were prepositions: words like 'in', 'on', 'to', 'for', 'from', 'with', 'by'. Check where they rate in the Top 20 tables on p. 47.

Prepositions are extremely versatile words. Over the centuries, prepositions have acquired a variety of uses.

Take the preposition 'for', for example. Look at the different ways this tiny, unassuming word can be used.

I have applied *for* a grant.
Do you take me *for* a fool?
We'll all feel a lot better *for* a holiday.
Have you got change *for* a tenner?
These chocolates are *for* you.
I am acting *for* my client.
She's good enough to play *for* England.
He is not very tall *for* his age.
The Lake District is famous *for* its scenery.
Australia were all out *for* 35 runs.
Keep right on *for* about ten miles.
I hope they're all home *for* Christmas.

Prepositions could be called map words. They help your mind map out where things are. Look at the following excerpt from a book of guided walks and spot the prepositions.

> At the junction with the Headrow turn left, passing the Horse and Trumpet pub, with its recently cleaned Victorian facade. Down a passage is the entrance to the City Palace of Varieties, a remarkable and nationally famous survival of a Victorian music hall. The original entrance was at the rear, on Swan Street. Turn into Land's Lane, where monotonous department store buildings of the 1960s have replaced the 17th century Red Hall. At the junction with Albion Place stands the Church Institute, now converted into shops and offices. On the other corner of Land's Lane is a new stone building in Victorian style. Albion Place has a fine run of Victorian and Edwardian buildings. On the south side... 9

activity

Choose an interesting short walk in your own locality. Make it interesting by the way you write it and pay particular attention to helping the reader find the things you are drawing attention to. For example:

> On your right, just past Bettabuys supermarket, you will see the entrance to a narrow alley. Go through the alley which leads into a small yard. Go up the steps at the far

side of the yard, taking a moment to look inside the old blacksmith's shop at the foot of the steps.

Idioms

The word 'idiom' comes from the Greek word for 'your own'. Idioms are the peculiar ways people have of using their own language, and are most likely to occur in speech. They are phrases whose meaning is not obvious from the meanings of the individual words. People who speak the language will know what the phrase means, but the meaning will not be obvious to foreign speakers. Two well-known examples are:

A change of heart
To foot the bill

Imagine the mental picture these idioms would conjure up for someone who knew the meaning of each word but had never seen the idiom before.

English contains a lot of idioms that are made up of grammatical words. What do these examples mean?

ifs and buts; off and on; ins and outs; whys and wherefores; with it; to and fro; yes and no; his and hers; this and that.

Grammatical words can also be tacked on to verbs to give verbs completely new meanings. There are thousands of these verbs in English. The grammatical words most often occur at the end of the phrase, but they can also occur at the beginning. Here is an example of how a verb can take on

gEt Ma
the gR n
h g a

extra meanings by the addition of grammatical words.

> *to go:* **ongoing; go off somebody; the fish has gone off; going out with; going up in the world; an outgoing person; go for it; days gone by; going on a bit; go over someone's head; go to it; mind you don't go under.**

The meanings of these phrases are idiomatic: you cannot work the new meaning out from the meanings of the individual words. People learning English find idioms difficult and need a lot of advice.

activity

There are whole dictionaries of idioms. Choose three from the 'to go' examples above and write an explanation of what they mean. Then choose one of the following verbs and see how many idioms you can make by adding grammatical words: to give; to make; to take; to put.

Grammatical words at work

Arguments and explanations

Whenever we are trying to explain something, put over our own point of view or argue with somebody else's explanation or point of view, we need to use grammatical words like:

> **'because', 'when', 'however', 'therefore', 'despite', 'unless', 'if', 'while', 'although';**

and phrases like:

> **'on the one hand', 'either...or', 'in spite of'.**

There are also many words that are valuable in explanations and arguments because they link ideas in the way we want them to be linked.

Many of these words are defined as adverbs in dictionaries but their function is grammatical, and often, 'seriously grammatical', that is, they can be used quite impressively and persuasively and are worth knowing. Here are some examples:

For starting explanations and arguments off:

> **First, In the first place, To start with, Initially, To begin with.**

For pressing on with:

> **secondly (etc.), furthermore, moreover, meanwhile, nevertheless, for instance, in other words, next, also, then, and so, accordingly.**

For concluding explanations and arguments:

> **thus, penultimately, finally, consequently, in conclusion, in the end, last of all.**

activity

An argument or explanation is something like a recipe or a set of instructions. It is best set out in clear stages.

Write an explanation of how something works, paying special attention to the words you use to take your reader from one stage to the next. Follow the example of the text about the dead man's handle on p. 25 but make sure you write about something you know very well.

When thinking about an argument, a point of view or course of action, it is useful to make two lists, headed by well-known grammatical words: *for* and *against*.

activity

Think about the arguments for and against such issues as capital punishment, or banning tobacco advertising, or scientific experiments on animals. Decide on your point of view and find arguments to support it.

Write an argument about something in which you believe strongly. Pay special attention to the logic of your argument. What is the connection between what you are saying, what has gone before and what is coming next?

Remember: grammar holds explanations and arguments together.

Texts

The following poem was written over 60 years ago, when typewriters were the best-known modern technology for processing words. To amuse his readers, the poet pretends that the poem has been written by a cockroach jumping from key to key on a typewriter. Because Archy (the cockroach) can only jump on one key at a time, he is unable to type capital letters. Some punctuation marks are impossible too, so he has left them all out!

i was talking to a moth
the other evening
he was trying to break into
an electric light bulb
and fry himself on the wires

why do you fellows
pull this stunt i asked him
because it is the conventional
thing for moths or why
if that had been an uncovered
candle instead of an electric
light bulb you would
now be a small unsightly cinder
have you no sense

plenty of it he answered
but at times we get tired
of using it
we get bored with the routine
and crave beauty
and excitement
fire is beautiful
and we know that if we get
too close it will kill us
but what does it matter
it is better to be happy

for a moment
and be burned up with beauty
than to live a long time
and be bored all the while
so we wad all our life up
into one little roll
and then we shoot the roll
that is what life is for

it is better to be a part of beauty
for one instant and then cease to
exist than to exist forever
and never be a part of beauty
our attitude toward life
is come easy go easy
we are like human beings
used to be before they became
too civilised to enjoy themselves

and before i could argue... 10

In your listening and reading:

- **look out for interesting uses of prepositions.**

- **pay special attention to sentences containing: 'if', 'unless', 'despite', 'although', 'because', 'nevertheless'.**

- **make a note of unusual combinations of verb plus grammatical word; for example, 'look forward' is well known but 'take forward' is a recent one favoured by some politicians.**

In your speaking and writing:

- **make sure your grammatical words are doing exactly what you want them to do (don't be vague).**

- **practise arguments that use words like 'although', 'moreover', 'however'.**

- **think about your punctuation with grammatical words.**

1. Which is the most frequently used grammatical word in the poem?

2. Find the sequence of words 'or why if that'. What on earth does Archy mean?

3. Look for the following grammatical words and explain why they are useful in arguments: why, because, if, but, than, before.

4. What lexical words tell you this poem was written by an American?

5. In order to understand this poem, you probably had to say parts of it aloud to work out what Archy is saying. Go through the poem carefully and put in all the missing punctuation. When you have done this, read it aloud to a partner so that it is clear what Archy means. Has your partner punctuated it in the same way?

6. You will have noticed that the poem is unfinished. Write the last verse in the way you think Archy would have written it.

EPISODE 4

[*The teenage turmoil from Oz is still going on. Charlene and Craig are back in their own rooms and talking over the telephone this time. Craig is dejectedly polishing his surfing trophies, while Charlene is absentmindedly piecing together torn up scraps of a photo of her and Craig. As she talks, she reconstructs the photo and then shreds the piece showing Craig's grinning face.*]

CHARLENE Are you still mad at me for last night?

CRAIG Now and then. Why?

CHARLENE What kind of answer is that?

CRAIG Well…

CHARLENE Well nothing Craig. I've had just about enough of this. Why don't you just spit it out. You want to finish with me but you're not man enough even to say it to my face…

CRAIG [*trying to explain*] If only… [*struggles to choose his words*]

CHARLENE If only you had the guts to admit it! Craig, it's over and you know it. Why have you never been able to say what you really feel?

CRAIG Because…because…

CHARLENE Go on – say it! Because you're a man, because you're an idiot. Because you've found someone else!

CRAIG [*getting angry*] Why…?

CHARLENE [*continuing in full torrent*] Well that's fine by me. There's plenty of other fish in the sea…and better looking ones too! Fish a girl can trust; fish who aren't afraid to say what they feel: honest, decent fish…

CRAIG [*looks utterly baffled*] What?

CHARLENE Craig? Are you still there?… [*to herself*] But then, was he ever really there for me?

CRAIG [*with determination*] Charlene. Since when…?

[*We hear the click of the receiver as Charlene slams down the phone.*]

No lexical words here for Craig. He has retreated into the safety of grammatical words, which make noises but cannot mean anything without the lexical words.

Continue the script so that Craig is making all the running and Charlene is the one using only grammatical words.

55

In this chapter you will investigate:

- **some important differences between spoken and written language;**

- **some of the distinctive features of spoken communication;**

- **some of the distinctive features of written communication.**

Humans are very clever users of language. They can speak it, listen to it, read it and write it. Frequently they do more than one of these at the same time. Everybody has had a conversation with one person while overhearing another, and it is not at all unusual for people to write while listening, for example, to the radio. It is perfectly possible to fill in a form, which involves reading and writing, while talking and listening to somebody as you are doing it. It makes demands on your concentration, but life frequently makes us do two or three things at once.

Humans also use language to think with. You can listen to the radio while thinking about events that happened to you yesterday. Your mind can be on something else while you are reading or writing your homework.

activity

Think about how you use language every day. Which do you do most, speaking, listening, reading or writing? Which do you do least? Which do you sometimes do at the same time?

The difference between speech and writing

activity

Read the following which explains how to change a computer disc:

> well – you've got to put your disc in first – that programs it, right? – see, there's your files come up on the screen – right – now take it out and put in your

floppy – that's right – no – hang on – you've got it the wrong way round – we'll mark this side so you'll know – right – put it back in – now you can save on this disc, right? – but don't forget to press F1 to tell it you've changed the disc – there – the screen's changed – looks a bit full to me, this – do you need all these files?

Nobody would fail to recognise this as speech that has been transcribed (that is, written down as spoken).

How do you think this text would be different if it were written down? Rewrite the piece so that it could be put in a handbook.

Brainstorm your ideas, as a class, on the differences between speech and writing. You could begin your lists as follows:

Speech	Writing
You can hear it	Is silent
Very impermanent (unless tape recorded)	Permanent (unless you burn it)
Less formal	More formal

Vox box

"I prefer to talk to people face to face when a serious matter occurs."

"Talking is more helpful than writing when you want to have an argument with somebody."

"With writing, you have time to think about it and use the kind of words you think are right."

"When you write, you can't show your emotions."

Body language

The combination of facial, hand and body signals and messages that makes up body language can sometimes say as much as the words themselves. It is a vital part of the repertoire, not just of actors, comedians and politicians, but of every speaker in any situation. Just try stopping your body language next time you have a conversation and see what happens.

activity

Watch a videotape of a TV discussion programme, say, an interview on a chat show, and then watch part of it with no

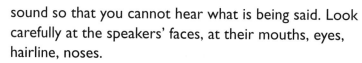

sound so that you cannot hear what is being said. Look carefully at the speakers' faces, at their mouths, eyes, hairline, noses.

What movements do you detect? What signals are they giving? How do you read or interpret their facial expressions? Can you guess what is being said? Can you tell how it is being said: light-heartedly? unpleasantly? seriously? anxiously? defensively? aggressively?

Try to identify just what gives you your impression. Remember that there are 400 muscles in the face that twitch, flex and relax in all sorts of different combinations as you speak.

Now replay the videotape with the sound on and note how facial expressions and spoken words work together to communicate meanings.

Follow this up with some real-life observation of people's faces during conversation. It is best not to do it during a conversation of your own as it will be very off-putting!

Try to identify what eyes, lip movements, grimaces, add to the words.

Humans also express themselves through hand signals, body posture and movement. Obvious examples are leaning forward, backing off, touching, waving arms about and the angle of the head.

activity

Look at your sample of videotape. This time, watch what people do with their hands during conversation, for example, pointing fingers, open palms, hands together, flicks and sweeps, clenched fist.

What do hand signals communicate? Write a list of the hand movements you notice.

Look at a different three minutes of video (it can be one person talking). Turn the sound off and try to read the hand signals in conjunction with facial expressions. Again, guess what is being said, and say how you think it is being said. Do the same for posture and body movement.

If your class collects its observations together you should be able to make a dictionary of body language used in spoken English.

Intonation

In addition to body language, humans have one other important system for communicating meanings, and that is intonation. Intonation is the rise and fall of pitch in the human voice and is closely linked to the rhythms of speech. You could call it the 'tunes' of speech, for every spoken sentence has a tune to it.

You've already seen in Chapter 1 how a statement can be turned into a question just by using intonation. Regardless of accent, voices seem to rise and fall for specific reasons, for example: for emphasis; to express feeling.

activity

Using evidence you have already collected, and new evidence where you need it (either from TV, radio or real life), decide what happens to intonation when people:

– ask questions;

– want to emphasise a word or phrase;

– exclaim;

– give commands that are polite/less polite;

– threaten or menace;

– are explaining something.

Now listen to your video samples and make a note of places in speech where voices:

– become louder or softer;

– rise or drop in tone;

– speed up or slow down;

– change in any other way.

Make some observations of different intonation features of speakers on the evening TV news. Listen also to how different radio DJs use their voices. Phone-ins are another interesting opportunity to observe intonation.

It is likely that your local dialect will be spoken with a recognisable accent. Listen carefully, and identify the distinctive ways in which people in your region speak.

So far you have looked at a wide range of support systems that operate when human beings talk and listen to each other. When you write, suddenly all these things are not there any more. Speech takes place between two or more people, whereas writing takes place inside your own head and then on a sheet of paper. Writing is quite a lonely activity by comparison, and when it gets to wherever and whoever it is going to, you and your body language and intonation won't be there to help it along. It will have to 'speak' for itself.

activity

Below is a list of features of everyday spoken language. Have a look at it, and then see how many you find in the spoken account that follows, which explains a minor boating mishap.

– fillers (ums and uhs)

– interrupted sentences

– unfinished sentences

– abrupt changes of topic

– backtracking (remembering something that occurred earlier)

– pauses

– confusion about pronouns (to whom or what do they refer?)

– frequent use of 'and'

   so I – er – well you know – I sort of swung it round too

hard and – and oh no before that I hadn't pulled back the throttle – well I thought I had – so I was going too fast – look there's one just like ours only without this awning thing – I think this is the trouble you know you can't see out properly – anyway it bumped and he went mad and he said get off the boat – there wasn't any damage – I got it in neutral and it cut out – I said I was sorry and I picked up all the things – but he's just not – er – well – I'm not his favourite person just at the moment [11]

If this account were written it would be different. Rewrite it for two different readers:

in a letter to a friend explaining about your mishap on holiday;

in a letter to the owner of the boat explaining and apologising.

The second letter will be more formal than the first, but even the first letter will be different from speech.

Pauses and punctuation

One of the things speech and writing have in common is the need for pauses, though pauses in speech are different from pauses in writing.

For example, writing puts spaces between the words, whereas there are frequently no pauses between spoken words. Pauses in speech are usually:

– to give the speaker time to breathe;

– to allow time to think;

– to create an effect on the listener, for example anticipation, or to get attention;

– to enable the speaker to cough, sneeze, laugh, groan, or do something else.

They can also occur because somebody has interrupted.

Check this out. Observe when, how, where and why people

pause in their speech. You may find other reasons than those listed above.

Pauses in writing, usually in the form of spaces and punctuation marks, are there to help the reader's eye. Punctuation is a signal system, a bit like the highway code. It makes the text easier to read and ensures that the reader gets the writer's meaning. It is very much connected with thinking rather than with speaking. Nobody, for example, speaks capital letters and full stops, because intonation, body language and context make it clear enough where sentences begin and end.

Activity

Choose what you think are the five most important punctuation marks in the English language. Write an explanation of the use of these punctuation marks for younger children, explaining why they are important.

, . ; : < > [ ] ( ) - * " ' ! ? /

Standard punctuation

English punctuation has a long and fascinating history. In the Middle Ages individual writers punctuated in whatever way they thought best, so there was a wide variation in the way punctuation marks were used. With the invention of the printing press, however, punctuation gradually became standardised. Even William Caxton, the inventor of printing in England, had his own system to begin with (see photo).

Most people know that sentences begin with capital letters and end with full stops. That's an elementary rule of the punctuation code. Question marks and exclamation marks are straightforward too.

The comma and the apostrophe are not quite so straightforward.

Investigating commas

You will no doubt have discovered that the comma is useful

62

for separating words when they need to be separated, as in a horizontal list for example:

They bought bread, cheese, fruit and cider for a picnic.

Notice that in lists of this kind the final comma becomes an 'and'.

Commas also have grammatical uses that make a difference to the meaning. They separate parts of sentences.

She is, you know, the best athlete in her year.
Although your trainers are a bit old fashioned, they are better than nothing.

activity

Sometimes, when you get really involved with your writing, it's easy to put a comma when you should have used a full stop. Here's an example:

We decided to climb the wall, it didn't take us long.

The passage that follows has had its punctuation marks deleted. Read it aloud to a partner and listen for where the natural pauses and emphasis should be. Discuss with your partner how the passage should be punctuated.

hard work can turn anybody into a musician and might even produce a mozart scientists claimed yesterday studies have found that the ability to play a musical instrument has almost nothing to do with any musical gift but everything to do with practice and encouragement at home john sloboda professor of psychology at keele university said it is a myth that some people can sit down at the age of five and play beautifully musicians are made not born even mozart had to put in the hours he said that recent studies had shown that if children accumulated about 5000 hours of practice before the age of 18 an hour and a half a day they should be good enough to get into music college. 12

Apostrophes

You can sometimes 'hear' commas in speech as pauses. This helps with writing. Apostrophes are not so easy to 'hear'. They usually show that something is missing, for example:

isn't, won't, didn't, can't

This process happens naturally in the way that we speak to each other and is not bad English. In writing, however, we are usually more formal.

Apostrophes also indicate that something or someone belongs to something or someone else. This different use of the apostrophe occurs in speech and writing:

John's car, Sally's book, the dog's tail, the horse's mouth, the horses' mouths

Texts

Below is a conversation between a group of comprehensive school pupils. The text is a transcript, which means that it is a copy in writing of everything recorded on audiotape. The initials of the speakers have been used, plus some punctuation. The brackets indicate a short pause.

P. no! it's important to everyone () to have friends () everyone needs to feel wanted don't they () to be popular?

K. mmm () for me the thing that I worry about most is whether or not people like me I don't like it when people don't like me

P. talk behind your back?

K. mmm I do not like it when people do that

J. some people don't really seem bothered () take the attitude () just take them as they are

K. yeah I always feel that's how I want to be and I want to be () let people think what they like I don't care and I don't () but I do not like it when people say stuff behind my back

S. yeah I don't either () but I don't really care if people aren't my friends if they can't take me the way I am then I don't want to be their friend anyway

J. they're not worth having

Now look at a scene from a script written for BBC TV by Michael Cahill. Eileen lives at home with her family, but thinks her friend, Deana, who lives in a small flat of her own, has a much better life. Jimmy is Eileen's brother.

The Living Room

Jimmy	*[noticing Eileen's mood]* **Hallo, sunshine!** *[chuffs her on the face, sparring playfully]*
Eileen	*[whacking his hand down]* **Stop it!**
Jimmy	**Who's upset you?**
Eileen	**No one!** *[Jimmy laughs as though to say "Not much".]*
Mother	**She's in a mood because she can't stay the night at some friend's place… Talk to her, Jimmy.**
Eileen	*[leaps up indignantly]* **That's it! "Talk to her"!**
Jimmy	*[leaps back, mock fear]* **Is that the girl you brought round to see us the other week?**
Eileen	**Yes, it is.**
Jimmy	*[to mother]* **We gave her a lift home and the car broke down on the way back.**
Eileen	**You can laugh, Jimmy, but you weren't timed with a blinking stop-watch before you were married! You did as you pleased!**
Mother	**She doesn't half lay it on thick.**
Jimmy	**I couldn't do as I pleased!**
Eileen	**As good as…**
Mother	**She won't see it that parents worry more about a girl than a boy.**
Jimmy	**I had to make sure Lena was back home at a certain time when we were courting.**
Eileen	**Oh, you don't understand… I can't do anything I want to!**

Writers and actors are very good at making dialogue sound as though it is 'real', but when you look closely at unscripted speech and scripted speech, there are some important differences.

Which of these two dialogues would actors find easier to act? Why?

What differences are there between scripted and unscripted

dialogue? What changes would you have to make to the first dialogue to make it fit as a conversational scene in a TV play?

Style

It is more than punctuation that accounts for differences between speech and writing.

Writing has to be much more explicit, more detailed than speech because it has to work on its own. There is a big difference of style between speech and writing.

Below is an advertisement for a Sanyo video recorder. It appeared in a magazine and is obviously a piece of writing. It is also dealing with technical information which means there will be a lot to take in. What is interesting is that the advertisers have deliberately tried to make the writing sound like a friendly conversation.

Read the text of the advertisement (opposite) and make a list of all the things that make it sound like speech rather than writing.

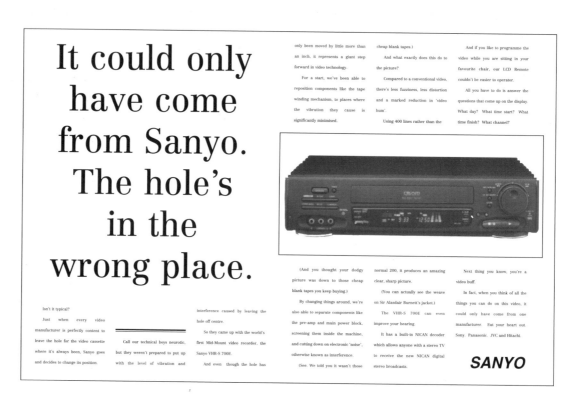

It could only have come from Sanyo. The hole's in the wrong place.

Isn't it just typical?

Just when every video manufacturer is perfectly content to leave the hole for the video cassette where it's always been, Sanyo goes and decides to change its position.

Call our technical boys neurotic (as we often do) but they simply weren't prepared to put up with the high levels of vibration and interference caused by leaving the hole off centre.

So they came up with the world's first Mid-Mount video recorder, the Sanyo VHR-S 700E.

And even though the hole has only been moved by little more than an inch, it represents a giant step forward in video technology.

For a start, we've been able to reposition components like the tape winding mechanism, to places where the vibration they cause is significantly minimised.

(And you thought your dodgy picture was down to those cheap blank tapes you keep buying.)

By changing things around, we're also able to separate components like the pre-amp and main power block, screening them inside the machine, and cutting down on electronic 'noise', otherwise known as interference.

(See. We told you it wasn't those cheap blank tapes.)

And what exactly does this do to the picture?

Why do you think the advertisers chose to write like this?

As a follow-up to the work you have just completed, keep these things in mind.

When you are reading:

- **make a note of unusual punctuation.**

- **look at the different ways writers have of handling dialogue.**

- **notice particular writing devices like subheadings and paragraphing.**

When you are writing:

- **check that you are not being too chatty.**

- **put yourself in the reader's mind, especially at the parts you think are important.**

- **proofread separately for punctuation, especially in longer sentences, by listening in your mind's ear for the pauses and the emphasis you want to communicate.**

- **check you are not tacking sentences together with commas, when full stops would be better.**

Soap and Away

EPISODE 5

Charlene is finishing with Craig. She is returning his things, but unfortunately the script hasn't been punctuated, making it difficult to read.
Put in some helpful punctuation.

CHARLENE   pulling items from the bag I think youll find thats everything all the things I borrowed your CDs tapes two T-shirts and your stupid surfing magazines theyre all there

CRAIG   youre making a big mistake Charlene

CHARLENE   no I dont think so I counted them

CRAIG   I dont mean my stuff I meant about you and me I want to say Im sorry and I think we should talk

CHARLENE   theres nothing to talk about is there isnt that what you said and anyway Ive come to the conclusion that being with you is a waste of valuable tanning time

CRAIG   cant you see I'm trying since weve been apart Ive learned that there really is more to life than…

Now finish the episode and the story in your own words.

Introduction

Decontextualised grammar exercises of the old school are rightly discredited with both teachers of English and teachers of linguistics. Their chief failing was their tendency to reduce language to something barely recognisable in real life and to oversimplify the flexibility of the language system.

Teaching grammar in the context of everyday and literary use has proved interesting and even quite lively. It can raise questions about human behaviour that are fascinating to explore. All kinds of issues to do with social class, gender bias, personal knowledge or the history of the language lie below the surface of humble pronouns, adverbs and prepositions.

The trouble with the decontextualised approach is that its 'system' becomes too rigid overall, making explanations about details slightly unconvincing; the trouble with approaches embedded in contexts is that the learner loses sight of the wood as each tree becomes more and more interesting.

What is needed for today's students is a semi-contextual approach in which their explorations of grammar can move in and out of contexts in the manner of good scientific learning, or learning a second language. They need to get a view of grammar that relates to life as well as to language.

This book has been devised to give students opportunities to explore key areas of English grammar in a way that is both systematic as well as experiential.

Chapter 1: Life sentences

It is important to get across to pupils that sentences are part of life as well as language. Communication cannot manage without them. We produce them intuitively, but being able to control their construction and effect gives more power in both speech and writing.

There is a popular assumption that speech is characterised by incorrect or improper sentences. Let the pupils discover that, for all sorts of good reasons, spoken sentences make perfect sense without being constructed as explicitly or as tidily as written sentences. Many linguists use the term 'utterance' when referring to spoken sentences. It's a good idea and much could be gained by pupils from contrasting speech that utters with speech that only mutters.

There are only four kinds of sentences and have only been four for thousands of years. Nobody in the foreseeable future is likely to invent a new one or cause one to be abolished. Greetings are the odd one to fit in because, like exclamations, they are so distinctive, perhaps even unique.

The best way for pupils to approach grammar topics is by considering use first and structure later. Some structural features you may wish to develop out of the work in this chapter are:

- the use of parenthesis either by brackets or pairs of commas;

- the occasional use for effect of one or two (no more) one-word sentences carefully placed in a narrative;

- the use of alternatives for 'and' and 'then' conjunctions, for example: although, whenever, despite, unless, if, however, moreover, all of which are subordinating conjunctions.

Rather than approach activities of this kind by exercises, a more linguistic approach would be for pupils to collect, from texts, examples of ways in which ideas in different parts of sentences are joined together or kept separate. Joining together or separating are exactly what punctuation is all about.

Punctuation is pre-eminently a grammatical topic.

Essentially, sentences are constructed and punctuated according to rhythms of thought, which is another reason that spoken utterances are so different from written sentences. Intonation (rhythmic and melodic rise and fall) is as powerful a communicator in speech as the actual meanings of words. A principal reason why writing is more difficult, and punctuation essential, is the absence of aids to communication like intonation, voice qualities, facial expressions, gestures. Pupils could explore how questions are conveyed in speech simply by a rising intonation on one word alone, for example: Coffee?

Pupils are often criticised, with justification, for writing too much in the way that they speak. A partial corrective to this is listening with the inner ear to the rhythms of written sentences. A good way to do this is by first listening to the effects of intonation in real speech. Pupils are good at transcribing brief stretches of conversation. They usually have good ears and are quite pernickety about getting it down on paper accurately. It's a good exercise for thinking about punctuation but it's even more valuable when they come to see how little a transcription tells you about all the nuances in a conversation. The transcript of the switchboard operators at Bristol Royal Infirmary is available, along with much more, in the LINC units (see p. 80). There is also a video available of the actual conversations, so that it is possible for pupils to transcribe a variety of short conversations and compare their versions with professional transcripts. This kind of close attention to the utterances of everyday life teaches more about sentences than the guidebooks to correct English.

Collecting sentences can be fun as well as instructive, especially if sources include greetings cards, comics, legally binding documents, jokes, things people say on the market, news bulletins, headlines, public notices, mottoes, and all kinds of famous sayings.

Often, in everyday conversation, speakers use one word sentences, for example: 'Yes.' 'No.' 'Hardly.' 'Why?' 'Rubbish!' All these, and many, many more, serve as one word responses or comments. They

work because the verb is implied, for example:

> **Yes.** = 'I agree.'
> **No.** = 'I don't agree.' or 'I won't.'

Sometimes a one-word sentence is an explicit but extremely concise verb form, for example:

> **Thanks.** = 'I thank you.'
> **Maybe.** = 'It may be so.'

One (and two) word sentences are sometimes used in writing but less frequently so, especially in continuous prose. Writing needs to be so much more explicit. The opening page of Charles Dickens's *Bleak House* is frequently cited as an example of artistic effect achieved by not conforming to general practice. He does in fact begin with a two-word sentence: 'Fog everywhere.' The 'was' is implied. In *Jurassic Park*, Michael Crichton also uses one word sentences to create drama and suspense.

Detective novels sometimes use very brief, verbless sentences to create a stylistic effect close to purposeful conversation, but also to convey information economically. Here is the opening of W.J. Burley's *Wycliffe's Wild Goose Chase*:

> **Thursday evening. Outside it was raining. The three men sat round the fire in well worn leather armchairs.**

The young writer of *The Dead Pigeon* narrative (see p. 25) uses a two word sentence very effectively in the middle of her narrative: 'It was.' Notice how the moving effect is almost lost without proper punctuation.

Texts

Using the eczema text as a good example, pupils could be asked to write a pamphlet of their own on an issue they feel strongly about and which ought to be more widely publicised. Make sure they think about using a variety of sentences.

Extension activity

Collecting great sentences from history, literature, TV, school life, sport, can be a lively way of focusing attention on the concept of a sentence. Examples could be displayed as mottoes, proverbs, slogans, or under such a heading as 'The things people say'.

They could even be sub-divided under such headings as:

Momentous questions
Amazing statements
Historic exclamations
Unforgettable commands

If the question of verbs crops up, take a statistical rather than a prescriptive look. Yes, it is true that 99% of sentences have one or more finite verbs in them, but there will always be some that beat the system in a particular context. The important thing is that they do one of the four sentence jobs.

Finally, the question of clauses. A clause is a thought in a one-clause sentence: 'The cat sat on the mat.' A compound sentence consists of two clauses (or simple sentences) joined together most often by 'and': 'The cat sat on the mat and the dog ate the bone.' A complex sentence contains at least one subordinate clause. This means that the connection is a bit more involved than just 'and': The cat sat on the mat when/while/before/after/because/despite the fact that/unless the dog ate the bone.

Chapter 2: Names and things

It is important to remember from the outset that the term 'noun' is the name for the grammatical job done by a particular word. Ninety-nine per cent of the time many words are likely to be used as nouns but that does not mean that they are nouns forever. It is easy for pupils to get the wrong idea, partly because of a lingering misunderstanding of 'parts of speech' grammar, and partly because dictionaries use the term 'noun' alongside many words. What a dictionary does is to define each word in terms of its grammatical use. Most pupils could get more from a dictionary if they were just a little more observant and a little more knowledgeable about what each entry contains.

Look at the entry for the word 'right' in a popular school dictionary, such as *The Oxford Study Dictionary*.

Notice how the definitions of meaning are given according to whether 'right' is being used as an adjective, a noun, a verb or an adverb.

The importance of names in life is reflected by the important place occupied by nouns in grammar. A language can do far more complex things than merely supply a seemingly endless stream of nouns, yet if it is not clear in any communication just what is being identified or pointed to, making meaning becomes extremely difficult if not impossible.

Pupils will find much to interest them in exploring proper nouns and the giving of names. There is considerable social significance in naming looked at as social behaviour, and there are all kinds of psychological factors that follow, e.g. name changes, nicknames, and the sense of personal identity. Birth certificates usually arouse lively interest but sometimes discretion may be required to avoid painful or embarrassing consequences. Pupils can trace their language autobiographies in all kinds of ways, looking at, for example, all the occasions when and where they wrote or signed their names, or when their names were recorded by somebody else. Interest in names seems universal and a few dictionaries of names, possibly on loan from the local library, will be a useful resource. Equally, pupils compiling their own dictionaries of important nouns in their own hobbies and special interests makes a useful contribution to their developing study skills.

Extension activity

Marketing a product usually involves considerable research and expense.

Designing a wrapper for a product, and choosing a name, is usually a successful activity, but exploring options and doing market research on potential names deserves thorough treatment. It involves consideration of images, connotations and pronunciation that are ideal topics for language investigations.

What are you marketing: a new biscuit? potato crisps? new pop magazine? a new shampoo?

Pupils will need to consider the target audience and what will appeal to that audience.

Should the name be trendy? down market? nice? naughty? tough? tender?

Design meetings could be conducted, not unlike those in the TV series accompanying this book.

Final results should be presented orally and visually to the whole class. In this way a number of attainments in formal and semi-formal speaking and listening could be assessed.

The aspect of nouns that is likely to cause uncertainty or disagreement is the classification 'abstract nouns'. Don't be put off by this, in the belief that there is a right answer somewhere but too elusive for classroom use. Let the pupils make decisions about how more or less abstract a noun seems to them. One comprehensive definition teachers could use to help further classification is: an abstract noun refers to an action, a concept, an event, a quality or a state. Concrete nouns, on the other hand, refer to an observable, touchable person or thing. Gerunds are the words that usually lead to puzzlement. The word 'running', for example, is so obviously physical and 'verbish' to most youngsters that to be told it can also be a noun seems to fly in the face of common sense. Yet if it is nothing else, grammar is essentially common sense.

In the following sentences, 'running' is being used as a gerund, i.e. as a noun derived from the verb 'to run':

Running keeps you fit.
There's running on the telly tonight.
The thought of running horrifies me.

Pronouns are not a particularly difficult concept or term to understand, but it is easy to overlook their significance in use. They are a set of 'closed' or grammatical words, finite in number. We do not lose any, nor do we invent new ones. 'Thee' and 'thou' have been discontinued in standard English and occur now only in dialect or deliberately unconventional use. In dialect speech they are usually contracted to 'thi' and 'tha'. They do not represent a different pronoun but are alternatives to 'you'.

In English grammar there are eight different kinds of pronouns:

personal: I, you, he, she, it, me, him, her, we, they, them, us
possessive: his, hers
reflexive: myself, herself
distributive: each, either
demonstrative: this, that
interrogative: who? what?
relative: who, that
indefinite: any, somebody

Some observations and investigations pupils could make concerning the use of pronouns are:

When is the pronoun 'one' used? By whom?

How is the pronoun 'you' used in advertising? Why?

When did poets stop using 'thee' and 'thou'? Why? Look also at Bible translations through the ages.

Explain what is meant by 'a little less "I" and a little more "we"'.

Adjectives and articles do not normally present teaching problems, though, again, there is more to be gained by observing them in use than learning their names and classifications. In fact, there is nothing like investigating their uses for learning the terminology in an incidental but more informed way.

The idea of placing adjectives before or after the noun they are describing is well worth investigating. The former is called pre-modification, the latter post-modification. Clearly one strategy influences the reader's or listener's mind before he or she knows what the person or thing is, which could be very persuasive.

Pupils could also investigate 'adjective overload' by trying it out in a paragraph of description, or in a line or two of poetry, or in a TV advertisement. They could also remove adjectives from a passage and ask somebody else to guess what they might have been. How predictable or original were they? This is also a good way of assessing how well they understand the term.

Note that adjectives can sometimes be used as nouns:

'You've got to take the rough with the

smooth.'
'**Will the accused step forward.**'

One issue of grammar that looks deceptively straightforward is the distinction between a phrase and a clause. Usually, clauses are defined as groups of words containing a verb, whereas phrases are groups of words that do not contain a verb. The problem here for teaching and learning is the dependence of these definitions on an understanding of verbs, especially finite ones, and on the ability to recognise some of the ways in which sentences are constructed. A good start can be made by considering a very frequently used kind of phrase, namely the noun phrase. They can be as short as 'the mad dog' (article + adjective + noun) and as long as 'the sinister looking, stone castle on the top of the hill, at the other side of the swiftly flowing river'. The fact that one phrase contains three words and the other twenty makes no difference to the fact that both can function as subjects or objects in sentences. Both can be substituted by the pronoun 'it'.

Inventing long noun phrases preceding the remainder of a sentence like '…is great', or following 'It is…', makes pupils extend their ideas and also gives them a feeling for the rhythm of English sentences. One of the reasons why the sentences of non-fiction texts are difficult to follow or to retain is the frequent use of long noun phrases as subjects, which often contain abstract nouns to add a further level of difficulty.

Finally, a note about language acquisition by young children, which will serve as a connector between the topic of nouns and the topic of verbs in the next chapter. Many researchers across European countries and in the United States have observed how frequently infants make nouns do the job of verbs in a very unconventional yet perfectly sensible way. Here are some examples in English:

> '**Broom me Daddy.**' = Pretend to sweep me up with the broom.
> '**Mummy chair me.**' = Put me in the chair, Mummy.
> '**Ball me.**' = Throw the ball to me.
> '**Don't teddy me.**' = Don't tickle my tummy with teddy.

Clearly young children have a larger noun vocabulary than verbs, but they have the grammatical wherewithal to make words normally used as nouns, act like verbs. With a bit of help from the family's collective memory, plus a bit of observation next time they baby-sit, pupils should not only enjoy the inventiveness of infants but learn something from it about versatility and flexibility in getting meanings across through language.

Chapter 3: Where the action is

Verbs are used in such a wide variety of communicative intentions and nuances that their grammatical description is inevitably complex, full of interrelations and sub-categories. The terminology can understandably seem forbidding, and there is a danger of never perceiving the underlying concepts that make language study worthwhile. The following grammatical notes and teaching suggestions offer an overview of the verb that has relevance to two prime concerns of English teachers: helping pupils toward syntactic maturity in their writing, and extending their active vocabulary. They are set out alphabetically but they are not intended as a glossary for brushing up on terminology. It's the concepts behind the terminology that matter. Being able to identify accurately whether any verb in question is being used, for example, actively or passively is an academic skill that will elude many pupils, but getting an inkling into why the active and the passive voices might be important in the way we use everyday language is within reach of most pupils. You may wish to explore one or more of the following ideas as extensions of the activities in the chapter.

Active/passive voice

The use of passive verbs creates different effects:

- impersonality: 'roads were laid, canals dug and bridges built';

- objectivity or distancing: 'it appeared to have been broken'.

Most verb constructions in speech and even in writing are active rather than passive. Following George Orwell's advice, 'Never use the passive where

you can use the active', we have tended to avoid, even mock the passive voice because of its tendency to wordiness and pomposity. It can also sound a bit starchy or 'cold fish', and worse, creates an impression of evasiveness. These attitudes are echoed by the American, William Zinsser, 'The difference between an active…and a passive verb style — in pace, clarity and vigour — is the difference between life and death for a writer'.

All this seems to suggest that the passive is going out of fashion. Maybe it is, if its general use now is compared with, say, Victorian times, or between the wars. It still has its uses, however, in scientific writing, in reports where there is considerable uncertainty and when we wish to convey more concern for the receiver of an action than the perpetrator, for example: 'The refugees had suffered many hardships.' There is more to the passive than evasion, for example: 'It got broke Miss.'

The contrast between concern and evasion is a good topic for exploration, as is the relative use of active/passive verbs to describe men and women in certain kinds of popular fiction.

Auxiliary verbs

Pupils find it illuminating to do an occasional statistical survey of the words we use. Apart from nicely combining maths and English, it provides good data and expertise for a piece of non-fictional writing. Auxiliaries crop up all over the place in English, doing all sorts of things. They are ideal statistical material. You can begin question sentences with them, signify future tense, express a nuance of meaning, for example: 'You *will* do as you're told!'

'To be' and 'to have' are the most popular auxiliaries, but 'to do' should also be included. It might be explored as an extension to work on 'to be' and 'to have' or as a favourite verb of many young children, especially in its past tense form, for example: 'We did eat ice cream.'

Gerunds

The gerund has an almost comic status in grammatical terminology. It is assumed to be mysterious and anyone who can immediately give an

example of one earns a new respect out of all proportion to the knowledge displayed. It is not at all abstruse, and is an ideal topic for linking knowledge about nouns with knowledge about verbs. A gerund is simply a noun made out of a verb, usually the present participle '-ing' form. The Children's Society slogan, 'What I need is a good listening to', is an example of a gerund. It is a characteristic of English to generate nouns in this way: eating, fishing, walking, talking, teaching, learning.

The infinitive

The infinitive is a handy technical term. It makes a useful label under which all the variant forms of a verb can be classified. But it does more than that. It can imply future time, as in the headline 'Teachers to receive substantial pay rise'. It is also very good for epigrams: 'To err is human, to forgive divine'; 'To know is to love'; 'To be or not to be'.

Try collecting, better still inventing, epigrams and mottoes for greetings cards, mini-posters and T-shirts, using paired infinitives.

Modal verbs

Modality, along with gerunds and phrasal verbs (see below), has always been regarded as a rather rarefied, advanced, grammatical topic. Nothing could be further from the truth. It is dead central to pupils' experience of everyday communication and it is their use, misuse and, more often than not, non-use of modal verbs that gets them into or out of trouble. Modals are vital communicators, signalling at different times, politeness, caution, permission, uncertainty, recommendation and need.

As with the active/passive distinction, they are ideal material for exploration through drama. The effect of the inflection that goes with a 'might' or a 'must' in speech in communicating degrees of friendship, bossiness, co-operation or cautious advice can be investigated in mock interviews, arguments and phone-ins.

Phrasal verbs

Phrasal verbs (sometimes called verb idioms) are a fascinating aspect of idiomatic English. There are so

many of them that they have large dictionaries of their own, usually compiled for people learning English as a second language. (The *Longman Dictionary of Phrasal Verbs* is a useful one.)

It is a topic best explored in groups, there are so many to collect. You could begin with a small group of verbs that form a group of one kind or another (e.g. drive, ride, walk, run) and then systematically attach prepositions at the beginning and end of each word to see which are used and which not. Then comes the difficult part! Explaining just what they mean, when invariably they cannot be taken literally. 'Run', for example, yields such phrasal verbs as these:

> **run down (a business)**
> **run up (a dress)**
> **run over (some figures, or a person!)**
> **run out of (sugar)**
> **run in (a car, or an offender)**
> **run on (car engine, writing)**
> **run off (some photocopies)**

Regular/irregular verbs

This is not a particularly difficult concept. The pupils have lived all their lives coping successfully with the peculiarities of irregular English verbs and some will now be learning foreign ones. A new context for them, however, is observing their use by young children. If a chart is put on the wall it will be full of examples by the end of term, collected from brothers, sisters, cousins and infants here, there and everywhere.

The topic also provides a good focal point for looking at English spelling, since many spelling mistakes occur in the irregular verb forms, as for example, sought/caught.

Tense

English verbs express gradations of time past, present and future in a variety of fine discriminations, for example: 'She *will have been* in the theatre and back on the ward by now', which manages to combine elements of past, present and future.

Pupils could work in pairs to construct a spectrum of time, ranging from the most distant past they can conceive to the most distant future imaginable. It doesn't matter how they go about this, so long as they produce some kind of time continuum.

Tense in English grammar does not reflect tidily our common sense about time. There is general agreement among linguists that English does not have a future tense in the same way that it has a past and a present tense, no matter whether the verb is regular or irregular. Past and present tenses are signified in the word itself, by an added ending for example, but the future tense is signified by the use of auxiliaries like 'will' and by the combination of the present tense with an adverb, for example: 'I am going tomorrow.'

Another topic to develop is the way in which adjectives are frequently formed from past and present participles of verbs: 'a wishing well', 'baked potato', 'fishing rod', 'burnt toast'.

The forms of verb tenses are an area where dialectal variations in grammar are particularly noticeable. Some examples are very familiar:

> **We was running.**
> **I seen her do it.**
> **It ain't mine.**
> **They be tomatoes.**

These are all examples of non-standard forms. They should not be regarded as sub-standard.

The question of standard English is by no means an easy one to tackle in a worthwhile way in the classroom. Spelling is about the easiest, least controversial way in, and appropriate choice of vocabulary is manageable under the heading of differences between speech and writing. Grammar is much more difficult because non-standard patterns are deeply ingrained in community life and family talk. If teachers wish to tackle the topic head on, non-standard verb forms provide a good focus, allowing pupils to recognise that a good deal of their English is perfectly standard.

Chapter 4: Seriously grammatical

Faced with a number of word classes, some of which contain an extended range of sub-divisions, and an

extremely elastic set of rules that govern the use of words, it is helpful to know that there are only two kinds of words in the English language: lexical words and grammatical words. Lexical words have 'obvious' meanings and are sometimes called 'content' words because their meaning has some substance or reference to the world at large. Grammatical words are sometimes called 'function' words because their meaning lies entirely in the job they do within a sentence. As demonstrated in the many meanings of a preposition like 'for' (see p. 49), grammatical words depend upon the lexical words they are controlling for any contextual meaning they may have. They exist to enable users of the language to make the lexical words do what they want them to do.

Along with the distinction between four different types of sentence, the terms 'lexical' and 'grammatical' provide pupils with a beginners' kit for language analysis. The trouble with the old fashioned parsing approach was that it introduced too much terminology too soon. Moreover, once you had parsed a sentence it was difficult to know what to do next (except perhaps parse some more sentences!).

The approach advocated here investigates what actually goes on in language as it is used, rather than reducing decontextualised samples to a set of labels.

One activity that deserves a prepared set of texts, readily available, is the replacement of deleted words. If, for example, a text has all the lexical words deleted, its reconstruction will be a different, longer and more problematical task than reconstructing a text with only grammatical words removed. Do not underestimate, however, the difficulties some pupils will have trying to think of an appropriate grammatical word for a syntactic structure they cannot recognise. The surprise, sometimes annoyance with themselves, when they see the original writer's strategy, confirms the value of this kind of activity for drawing attention to varieties of sentence structure unfamiliar to them.

Word deletion texts do not all need to be prepared by the teacher. Pupils learn as much, if not more, through making their own deletions and seeing how other pupils respond.

Grammatical words tend to act as hinges or chain links in the syntax and are therefore a suitable point for looking at writing style. The most frequent criticisms of writing by 11 to 15 year olds are:

- lack of sentence variety;

- too much reliance on 'and', 'then' and 'but' connections;

- imprecise syntax;

- use of half sentences for full;

- misuse of the comma as an all-purpose splice;

- uncertain connection (cohesion) between one sentence and the next.

These are all criticisms at sentence level which can be addressed by paying some attention to key structural words ('although', 'whenever', 'despite'). It is easy to take these aspects of vocabulary for granted in the search for a more extensive lexical vocabulary. There is, however, no guarantee that because pupils know them they will use them effectively.

The chief aim of this chapter is to raise a general awareness of the use of grammatical words in everyday speech and writing. A wide range of social situations will provide opportunities for observation and further investigation. Here are some suggestions:

- the use of 'but' as an interrupter or a starter (or both) in conversations;

- the emphasis of volume or significant pausing on key words in an argument or sequence of explanation: 'and so', 'therefore', 'yes, but', 'however';

- beginning sentences with words that create expectation, and which inevitably generate a two-part sentence: 'although', 'if', 'unless', 'because' (remember that words such as 'although', etc., have a kind of built-in comma that has to appear somewhere in the sentence);

- the interpersonal effects of using pronouns like 'I' and 'you';

- the impersonal, often uncertain effect of using the impersonal 'it', as in 'I know, this is it!'.

Finally, there are one or two interesting aspects of grammatical words that are worth considering, if you are going to encourage pupils' investigations.

Pronouns

While classed as grammatical words, pronouns substitute for lexical words. Once you know who the pronoun stands for, in a story or a report, it becomes more substantial. Children observe this and often find it difficult to think of a pronoun as having no meaning in itself. This by no means subverts the terminology; it just means that children are better linguists than they are usually given credit for. One way to explain this effect is to liken pronouns to shirt buttons, or any other little object that will substitute for a lost chess piece. Once the two players have agreed on it, the shirt button is no longer anonymous but becomes a white knight.

Pronouns on their own are interesting to explore. The use of the pronoun 'you', especially in advertising and political persuasion creates a very direct communication.

Adverbs

This is a class of words that has a number of specifically grammatical functions. Consequently there is some overlap. Many adverbs have quite obviously lexical meanings; the '-ly' ones come to mind immediately, though it is difficult to say just what the content is of intensifiers like 'very' and 'really'. The interrogative words are classed as adverbs, but their function is usually grammatical except in instances where 'why', for example, is used as a plural noun in 'the whys and wherefores'.

'Who', on the other hand, can be classed as a pronoun in that it asks 'which person'.

Adverbs are frequently used to slant the way in which a whole sentence will be received. The '-ly' adverbs are particularly useful for this. For example:

> **'Actually,...', 'Basically,...', 'Incredibly,...', 'Hopefully,...'.**

Note the placing of the commas before the sentence actually (!) begins.

Adverbs have a lot of grammatical work to do

signifying time and place, which is why they overlap particularly with prepositions. Don't be dismayed by this; it is yet another instance of the language doing its best to express the range of meanings humans want it to express. In the section on verbs, for example, it was shown how the future tense can be expressed in English by means of the present tense plus an adverb like 'tomorrow'. Note too that the word 'tomorrow' is an adverb with lexical as well as grammatical uses.

When pupils explore words used for other than lexical meaning, they will include many words used as adverbs, for example: 'more', 'too', 'such', 'so'.

They will also notice adverbial phrases such as: 'for instance', 'and so on', 'in the second place'. The important thing is to recognise that they are looking at the intriguing complexities of the language, which is a far better learning experience for young language users than knowing the 'correct' but sometimes arguable classification of a particular word or phrase.

Chapter 5: Writing talk

Investigating some of the differences and connections between speech and writing is an essential part of learning to write. It generates and develops a range of awareness:

- that the absent reader has somehow to be kept in mind, for example, by rehearsing a dialogue in the mind prior to informative writing, or by making contact now and again during storytelling;

- that punctuation helps to avoid ambiguity and clarify meaning;

- that grammatical constructions need to be more explicit;

- that ideas, descriptions and events need to be elaborated if the reader is to appreciate what the writer has to say;

- that choice of vocabulary needs to be more precise in writing;

- that style in writing ranges between the semi-formal to the formal depending on audience, purpose and context;

- that the immediate opportunities for correction and alteration, or for backtracking, must be compensated for in writing by careful proof-reading.

In short, writers have to be simultaneous readers. Writing is putting thoughts and feelings into words. Talk, with all its dialectal and accentual features, is closer to thought, and frequently interferes, often for good, but sometimes off-puttingly for the reader, who does not expect to be taking part in an informal and inevitably one-sided conversation. More often than not, colloquialism takes advantage of readers who cannot answer back.

Punctuation is sometimes misunderstood as a reflection of speech patterns. It is true that saying a prospective sentence aloud helps to get the construction right and the comma in the proper place. But punctuation is essentially a device to point out grammatical construction. The seventeenth-century playwright, Ben Jonson, with his marvellous ear for contemporary speech, was nevertheless the first writer on English grammar to insist on this. Rhetoric is for speakers and listeners, punctuation for readers. Punctuation reflects the rhythms of thought. In a former age, sentences tended to be long, carefully balanced, or short and epigrammatic. Colons and semi-colons were the stock in trade of self-consciously literary prose. In our own day, sentences have grown generally shorter and more asymmetrical than, say, those of the eighteenth century. Different ways of thinking have intervened; different kinds of writing have developed.

There is no doubt that time spent on the various uses of the comma generates more understanding about punctuation than trying to cover all the punctuation marks superficially. Ironically, the one practice that does reflect speech is the use of the comma splice, often by children, to tack on afterthoughts that would be better as new sentences or embedded clauses. For example:

> **'The horse bolted from the yard, it was frightened, it didn't know where its mistress was.'**
> **'Great glowing and flashing lights fill the sky, this is the aurora borealis, it can only be seen at the North Pole.'**

There is a directness as well as an immaturity in this kind of writing that continues well into the GCSE years and occurs often on examination papers.

It is worth investigating, not as an error, but as a halfway house between speech and writing. What are the alternatives?

Exploring ways in which thoughts are put into writing is an appropriate context for also considering why there is such a thing as standard English.

The disadvantages or the unsuitability of non-standard verb forms, regional vocabulary and more widely used slang, in writing that is not specifically personal, are fairly obvious to most youngsters. Standard grammatical forms are the norm for most if not all writing, not because they are best but because they are conventional across a wide range of variations. It is difficult enough communicating in writing without added complications. But written standard English is not necessarily good English. There are lots of examples of barely comprehensible, alienating and desperately boring writing that uses standard English throughout. It is unlikely, however, that you will find good writing that is not in standard English, even when, as in a novel, the writer is deliberately using non-standard forms in dialogue.

Making a class anthology of short pieces (sometimes just sentences) that pupils consider to be good writing is one way of encouraging a more knowledgeable ear and eye for English prose at its best. Such an anthology ought to include pupils' own writing, since it is regrettable that many have the idea that good writing is something other people do.

Finally, teachers, if they have not already done so, will find the sections headed, 'The Writing Process' and 'The Writing Repertoire' in the LINC materials especially useful (see p. 80).

The units also contain much else on grammar that is relevant to the work in this book and in the accompanying TV programmes. They are not difficult to get hold of, but the unusual circumstances of their publication make them unavailable through normal commercial channels. In case of difficulty, contact the author of this book at the School of Education, University of Leeds.

An overview of grammar

The approach to grammar demonstrated in this book concentrates on functional aspects of grammar and relates knowledge about grammar to pupils' own uses of language in speech and writing. Teachers interested in the underlying theoretical framework may find the following summary useful.

English grammar consists of two main sub-divisions: morphology and syntax.

MORPHOLOGY is the study of the principles and practices whereby individual words can be changed grammatically, for example: adding suffixes to make plurals, to change tenses and to make, say, a verb into a noun. The structure of a word reflects grammatical functions, for example, 'action' is normally a noun while 'actioned' (whether you like the word or not) shows it is being used as a verb. Notice what differences of meaning are conveyed by the morphological variations in the following: Nationalised Curriculum; Nationwide Curriculum; International Curriculum.

SYNTAX is a description of all the principles and practices that enable words to be combined into grammatical units, for example, clauses and sentences. Traditional grammar also uses the term 'phrase' which denotes a unit of language of two words or more but not containing (or implying) a verb, for example, 'a fast car', 'beautiful dreamer', 'fish and chips', 'an apple', 'ins and outs'.

WORD CLASSES link morphology and syntax because they define the grammatical function of any word in its given place in a clause or sentence. The two overriding word classes are **LEXICAL WORDS** and **GRAMMATICAL WORDS**. The word classes subsumed under these are nouns, verbs, conjunctions, etc. Individual words tend to be used most often in one class but can also be used in other classes. Remember that it is the grammatical functions and the context of the whole sentence that will determine the class in which a word is functioning at any given time.

The **CLAUSE** is a basic 'thought unit' of English grammar. It contains a finite verb and corresponds to a **SIMPLE SENTENCE**. A **COMPOUND SENTENCE** is a combination of two or more simple sentences; a **COMPLEX SENTENCE** has at least one other clause dependent on the main clause.

Sentences are made up of **SUBJECTS**, **MAIN VERBS** (or **PREDICATES**), **OBJECTS** (**DIRECT** and **INDIRECT**) and **ADJUNCTS** (any other bits).

Because of the fundamental role of the verb, clauses (simple sentences) can be classified into different types according to how the verb is used.

Surprisingly there are only seven clause types:

1. **SV** e.g. The girl laughed. (Note that these clauses use **INTRANSITIVE** verbs.)
2. **SVO** e.g. The boy kicked the ball. (Note use of **TRANSITIVE** verbs.)
3. **SVC** e.g. Everybody seems happy.
4. **SVA** e.g. The school is in the country.
5. **SVOO** e.g. The boy gave the girl a kiss.
6. **SVOC** e.g. Their good fortune made them overconfident.
7. **SVOA** e.g. The girl smacked the boy across the face.

   S=subject; V=verb; O=object; C=complement; A=adverbial.

Note: complement refers to words that complete the meaning of the verb, adverbials are words and phrases that modify the action of the verb.

Transitive means that the action directly affects or interacts with an object. Intransitive means that it doesn't; it stands alone.

Transitivity is an important concept in life as well as in language, as are the concepts active and passive. Remember that some verbs can be both, e.g.: 'The children played' and 'The children played football'.

79

References

I Life sentences

1. *LINC Materials for Professional Development* (1992).

2. *LINC Materials for Professional Development* (1992).

3. Kay Macdonald, Bury College.

4. D.A. Bernstein *Psychology* (Houghton Mifflin Co, 1994).

2 Names and things

5. *LINC Materials for Professional Development* (1992).

6. *How Things Work* (Harper Collins, 1972).

7. William Shakespeare *Henry V* (Act V, Scene ii).

3 Where the action is

8. Cheshire Language Centre (1993).

4 Seriously grammatical

9. Janet Douglas and Ken Powell *Three Architectural Walks* (The Victorian Society, 1984).

10. Don Marquis *Archy and Mehitabel* (Faber and Faber).

5 Writing talk

11. Cheshire Language Centre (1993).

12. *The Independent*, 1 September 1993.

For further information on English grammar, consult:

- The *LINC Materials for Professional Development*, (especially Section 11 and the glossary)

- *Rediscover English Grammar*, by David Crystal (Longman, 1988)

- *A Reference Guide to English at A and AS level*, by B. and G. Keith (Longman, 1991).

- *The Oxford Companion to the English Language*, ed. by Tom McArthur (OUP, 1992).

Acknowledgements

Acknowledgement is due to the following whose permission is required for multiple reproduction:

Janet Douglas/Ken Powell/Victorian Society: extract from *Three Architectural Walks* (Victorian Society 1984); *The Independent*: extract 1 September 1993; Longman for extract from *Longman Concise English Dictionary* (1985 ed); LINC 1992 *LINC Materials for Professional Development* (Department of English Studies, University of Nottingham); Kay Macdonald, Bury College: eczema extract; Houghton Mifflin Co/D. A. Bernstein: extract from *Psychology* (Houghton Mifflin Co, 1994); Jonathon Green/Bloomsbury: extract from *Dictionary of New Words* (Bloomsbury 1993); HarperCollins: extract from *How Things Work* by The Bibliography Institute; Helicon for extracts from the *Hutchinson Encyclopedia*; Cambridge University Press/David Crystal: extract from *Cambridge Encyclopedia of Language* (1987); Gail Howe, Moor End High School, Crosland Moor: text transcript; Sanyo UK Ltd: advertisement text.

Photo credits

The Advertising Archives *p. 21*; BBC (taken from the *Get the Grammar* series) *pp. 5, 13, 16, 22, 36, 45, 48, 49, 53, 68*; British Film Institute *p. 27*; British Library *p. 62 IB 55005*; The Children's Society *p. 40*; Martyn Chillmaid *pp. 24, 38, 58, 59*; Hulton Deutsch Collection *p. 42*; Multiple Sclerosis Society *p. 41*; Nestlé UK Ltd *p. 23*; Sanyo UK Ltd *p. 66*.